Ōtautahi Christchurch Architecture

A Walking Guide

John Walsh
Photography by Patrick Reynolds

MASSEY UNIVERSITY PRESS

In memory of Sir Miles Warren
1929–2022

CONTENTS

INTRODUCTION

This book is the second, enlarged edition of a guide to a century and a half of Christchurch architecture, presenting outstanding examples of the various styles that have been in vogue, and introducing the significant architects who have practised in the city. It focuses on the centre of the city — the area bounded by the 'Four Avenues': Bealey, Fitzgerald, Moorhouse and Deans — and the important architectural site that is the Ilam campus of the University of Canterbury. This is where the city's most significant buildings can be seen and, in many cases, visited.

Of New Zealand's four main cities, Christchurch is the most conscious of its architectural history, or rather, its architectural traditions. Such civic awareness made the loss of much — but by no means all — of Christchurch's architectural legacy in and after the earthquakes of 2010–2011 even more poignant, and the debates about reconstruction even more pointed. This is a city that cares about its buildings.

The history of Christchurch architecture is a coherent and legible narrative, or at least it was before the earthquakes. It dovetails with the wider story of the city's gestation and development; from the start, Christchurch's architecture has been a key component of the city's Anglocentric brand. Christchurch began as an intentional city: it was founded in the 1850s by people with a vision for an ideal settlement and a plan for its realisation. That plan really *was* a plan — a grid imposed on a stretch of flat land (and on other people who had long used that land, of which more later). Christchurch was conceived as an Anglican colony, a transplanted cross-section of English society, and the settlers wasted no time in replicating the institutions of established Victorian order and in constructing the buildings to house them.

The regnant architectural style of the settlement moment was Gothic Revival, which was closely associated with High Church Anglicanism in mid-nineteenth-century England. Gothic Revival was the original style of the Christchurch settlement and dominated the religious, governmental and institutional architecture of the city until the end of the nineteenth century.

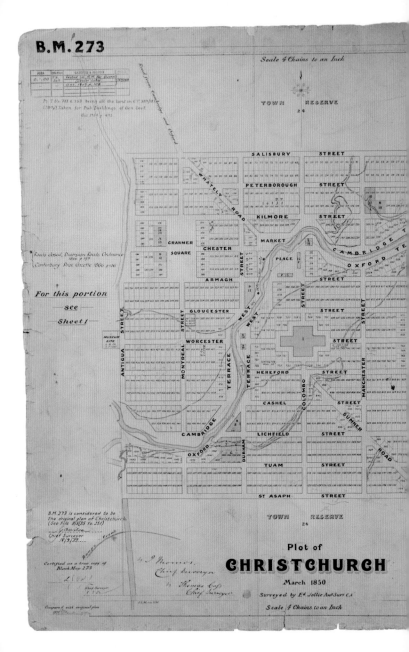

B.M. 273

Scale 4 Chains to an Inch

TOWN RESERVE
24

Pt. T.Ss. 701 & 763 being all the land in C.T. 389/57
(397a) Taken for Pub. Buildings of Gen.t Govt.
See 1960 p 491

SALISBURY STREET

PETERBOROUGH STREET

KILMORE STREET

MARKET PLACE

CHESTER STREET

CRANMER SQUARE

ARMAGH STREET

Roads closed, Diversion Roads Ordinance
1860 p 159
Canterbury Prov. Gazette 1860 p 96

For this portion
see
Sheet 1

GLOUCESTER STREET

WORCESTER STREET

HEREFORD STREET

CASHEL STREET

CAMBRIDGE STREET

LICHFIELD STREET

OXFORD

TUAM STREET

St ASAPH STREET

CAMBRIDGE TCE

OXFORD TCE

WHATELY ROAD

ANTIGUA STREET

MONTREAL STREET

DURHAM

COLOMBO STREET

MANCHESTER STREET

SUMNER ROAD

B.M. 273 is considered to be
the original plan of Christchurch.
(See File B/3(55 to 251)
J. Marlow
Chief Surveyor
31/7/71

Certified as a true copy of
Block Map 273

Compared with original plan

J. Thomas
Chief Surveyor

Thomas Cass
Chief Surveyor

TOWN RESERVE
24

Plot of
CHRISTCHURCH

March 1850

Surveyed by Ed. Jollie Ast Surv C.E

Scale 4 Chains to an Inch

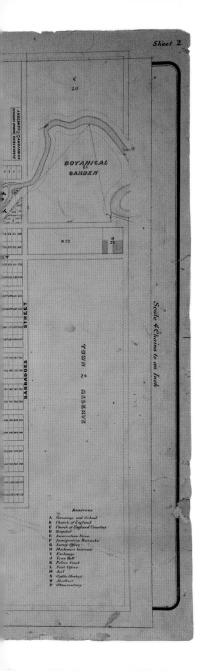

The original survey map — or 'Black Map' — of Christchurch, produced in 1850 by surveyors Joseph Thomas and Edward Jollie for the settlement's promoter, the Canterbury Association. The town grid was later extended north, south and east into the areas designated in the map as Town Reserve and now comprises the inner-city district known as the Four Avenues. The other border of the Four Avenues runs along the west side of Hagley Park, the large public park that spreads out from the empty area on the left side of the 1850 map. On the upper right of the map, land is set aside for a Botanical Garden; this was established in the parkland to the west of the grid in the 1860s.

The style's leading local exponent was Benjamin Mountfort (1825–1898), a figure who towers over the first 40 years of Christchurch architecture. (Eleven of the buildings in this guide were totally or partially designed by Mountfort.) Christchurch architecture has had two outstanding eras, periods in which the city's two greatest architects were producing their best work and, at the time, the best buildings in the country. Mountfort's Gothic Revival heyday, from the mid-1860s to the mid-1880s, was the first period of Christchurch architectural pre-eminence; the second was the years from the mid-1950s to the early 1970s, when Miles — later Sir Miles — Warren (1929–2022) was engaged in his Modernist, Brutalist phase.

Mountfort had able contemporaries, if not peers — architects such as ecclesiastical specialist Robert Speechly, a short-term migrant; Frederick Strouts, among other things a captain in the Canterbury Yeomanry Volunteers; and William Barnett Armson, Christchurch's prototypical successful architect-businessman. Warren, too, had talented contemporaries, none more important than his long-time practice partner, Maurice Mahoney. From the 1950s through the 1970s, Christchurch had a strong Modernist architectural scene, populated by architects such as — to cite just those whose work features in this book — Paul Pascoe, Humphrey Hall, Keith Mackenzie, Holger Henning-Hansen, and the architects who worked in anonymity for the Ministry of Works.

And then there was Peter Beaven. Like planets in a small solar system, Beaven and Warren spun in orbits that sometimes came into volatile proximity. Perhaps a chivalric analogy is more appropriate: especially in the twilight of their careers, Warren and Beaven often jousted over Christchurch heritage and urban issues, one entering the lists as a knight of the realm, the other as an indomitable Don Quixote.

A ribbon of design talent runs through the history of Christchurch architecture, connecting the eras of Mountfort and Warren. In the 80 years from late-career Mountfort to early-career Warren, the city's most notable architects were Samuel Hurst Seager and Cecil Wood. John Collins and Richard Harman had long careers in the decades before the Second World War, and the England and Luttrell brothers were also prominent in the early twentieth century. Between Gothic Revivalism and Brutalist Modernism, Christchurch architects sampled the regularly replenished smorgasbord of styles on offer in the Anglophone world. The city was treated to buildings in the Italianate, Collegiate Gothic, 'Tudorbethan', Queen Anne Revival and neo-Georgian styles, before Art Deco and Spanish Mission made their appearance. Continuity amidst this change was provided by a tradition of masonry construction and a genealogical design consciousness. Even as central Christchurch became a city of concrete Modernism, its architects alluded to its days of neo-Gothic stone, adding pointy bits to Brutalist buildings.

Some of the most important buildings from the 1860s to the 1970s have been carefully restored after the 2010– 2011 earthquakes: the Great Hall and the Clock Tower at the Christchurch Arts Centre, for example, the Memorial Dining Room at Christ's College, and Christchurch Town Hall. Other historic buildings have gone forever, most notably the Italian Renaissance-style Cathedral of the Blessed Sacrament (Francis William Petre, 1905), with its dome that evoked the Duomo (in Florence, that is).

History, even aside from seismic events, has not been kind to Christchurch buildings designed between the end of Modernism and the eve of the earthquakes. Post-modern architecture was always a bit of a freak show, everywhere, but Christchurch got off comparatively lightly. Instead, the city's architectural problem, in the late twentieth and early twenty-first centuries, was the increasingly moribund condition of the inner city.

Though a planned city, Christchurch was never a compact one; it had a big footprint for a relatively small population and so many low-rise and low-return commercial buildings that it was impossible to properly maintain them. With a few exceptions, if you wanted to see good new architecture in Christchurch in the millennium-ending decades, you headed to the suburbs to look at houses.

The years immediately following the earthquakes were difficult and often dismaying for the citizens of Christchurch. Things in the central city, though, have improved, and notably so in the three years since the publication of the first edition of this guide. There are still many gaps in city streetscapes and a profusion of empty lots, and a rash of tilt-slab concrete and glass buildings has provided critics with an itch to scratch, but the government investment in 'anchor' projects and the local determination to save significant heritage buildings are reviving the central city. The quality of many of these buildings, both new and conserved, not just in a design sense but also in terms of environmental and social performance, is a cause for civic optimism.

It is not a coincidence that the raising of architectural consciousness in Christchurch is contemporaneous with the increasing prominence in the city's economic life of the local iwi, Ngāi Tahu. Christchurch was established in a place that already was a place — Ōtautahi —and the wealth of Canterbury Province stemmed from the 1848 alienation, via a payment of £2000, of 20 million acres of Ngāi Tahu land. No Māori iwi has been more successful than Ngāi Tahu in using the Waitangi Treaty settlement process to develop the economic resources necessary to influence not just the politics but also the shaping of a city. As some of the projects in this guide indicate, Ngāi Tahu are regaining their naming rights to Ōtautahi, and design influence is starting to follow.

On the subject of inclusivity, there is another point to make. Readers of this guide will not fail to notice that it is a chronicle of the works of white males — not all of them dead — or, at least, of architectural firms they led. Architecture was traditionally a hierarchical as well as a gendered profession. (It remains stratified, although its workforce is becoming more diverse.) The guide, for reasons of consistency and concision, has followed the eponymous conventions of architecture practices, while acknowledging that such observance saves only a minority from what the great English historian E. P. Thompson called the 'enormous condescension of posterity'.

WALKING ROUTES

This footpath guide to the architecture of central Christchurch is organised into six walking routes: Park Side, which includes buildings in or near Hagley Park; River Side, which takes in buildings within a block of the Ōtākaro Avon River; East, which focuses on the area around ChristChurch Cathedral and the East Frame; South, the rapidly developing district below Lichfield Street; North, the blocks above Armagh Street; and Ilam Campus, the greenfield Modernist site of the University of Canterbury.

All of the buildings in the guide can be viewed from the street or other public areas. Many are open to closer inspection, and between them offer a variety of cafés, restaurants and bars.

Many of the buildings in this guide are listed as Historic Places (Category 1 or 2). These appellations are applied by Heritage New Zealand, the government agency that identifies New Zealand's important historical and cultural heritage sites. Category 1 Historic Places are those of special or outstanding historical or cultural significance; Category 2 Historic Places have historical or cultural significance (but are not so special). It should be noted that heritage listing does not assure heritage protection. The latter is dependent upon — but, again, not guaranteed by — 'scheduling' or listing in the district plan of the relevant local council.

ROUTE 1: PARK SIDE

Much of the Arts Centre complex can be explored; there are several cafés and restaurants in and around the site, and a hotel in the old Observatory. Ravenscar House Museum is open every day, as is Canterbury Museum, which has a café. Christ's College offers guided tours of its campus (check the school's website). In the Christchurch Botanic Gardens, the Visitor Centre is open to the public every day (and has a café), as is the adjacent Cuningham House conservatory.

ROUTE 2: RIVER SIDE

Christchurch Art Gallery Te Puna o Waiwhetū and Toi Moroki Centre of Contemporary Art (CoCA) Gallery are open every day, with cafés on site. Te Hononga Christchurch Civic Building is open to the public on weekdays. Oi Manawa Canterbury Earthquake National Memorial is designed as a site to be walked through and the Bridge of Remembrance is a pedestrian thoroughfare. The Church of St Michael and All Angels has regular Anglican services; The Terrace is a lively strip of bars and restaurants; and the former Public Trust Office Building has a rooftop bar/restaurant.

ROUTE 3: SOUTH

Hine-Pāka Christchurch Bus Interchange is a public waiting, if not loitering, space, and Te Omeka Justice and Emergency Services Precinct is open to those encountering the law and its agencies. Atlas Quarter is accessible to pedestrians and is in a neighbourhood replete with bars and restaurants, as is Boxed Quarter. The former A. J. White's building contains retail stores and the former Post and Telegraph Office has a café. The internal courtyard of the Stranges and Glendenning Hill Building shelters various hospitality venues.

ROUTE 4: EAST

Te Pae is Christchurch's convention centre, and accessible if you are a conventioneer. New Regent Street is a public street lined with cafés and restaurants. Isaac Theatre Royal stages performances, which may be booked on the venue's website. Tūranga Christchurch Central Library is open to the public every day, and is a very popular venue; there is a café on the ground floor. ChristChurch Cathedral is undergoing a complete restoration that is scheduled for completion in 2027. Old Government Building is now a hotel, with a public bar. The 'Cardboard' Cathedral is open to the public during the week, and to Anglican worshippers on Sundays. (The website lists opening and service times.) The various components of the East Frame medium-density housing can be viewed from Huanui Lane and Rauora Park. Tākaro ā Poi Margaret Mahy Family Playground is designed for children but welcomes visitors of all ages. Oxford Terrace Baptist Church welcomes members of that confessional group to its services.

ROUTE 5: NORTH

Christchurch Town Hall is a performance venue. (Tickets may be booked on the Town Hall website.) St Mary's Convent (Rose) Chapel is now run as an events venue. Knox Church is open to Presbyterian worshippers and, no doubt, other sympathetic believers on Sundays. (Details on the church's website.) Victoria Clock Tower is on a traffic island but can be reached on foot.

ROUTE 6: ILAM CAMPUS

The University of Canterbury's Ilam campus is publicly accessible. Not all buildings are open to visitors, but there are cafés at various sites, including Rehua and the Ernest Rutherford Building.

ROUTE 1: PARK SIDE

The planned foundation of Christchurch bequeathed two great legacies to the city: in the natural environment, Hagley Park and the Botanic Gardens; in the built environment, Gothic Revival architecture. This route along the west side of the CBD includes two of the strongest architectural compositions in Aotearoa New Zealand: the buildings around Christ's College quadrangle and the former Canterbury College buildings that now constitute the Arts Centre. Most of the late nineteenth- and early twentieth-century Arts Centre buildings have been impressively restored after suffering significant earthquake damage. The route takes in several buildings in the Botanic Gardens, the city's museum and a contemporary take on an unusual building type — the house museum.

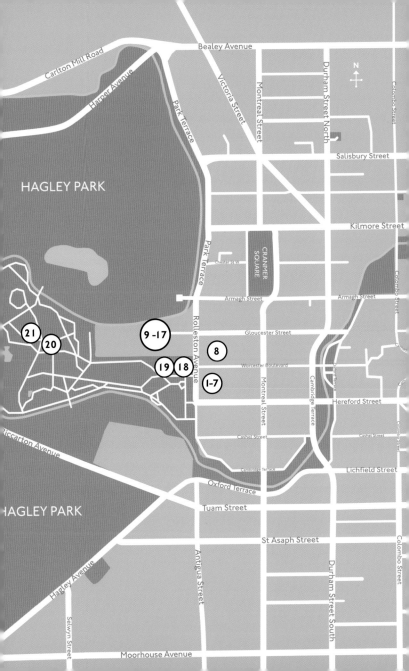

The Arts Centre
Te Matatiki Toi Ora

The Arts Centre Te Matatiki Toi Ora is a complex of 23 buildings, 21 of which are listed as Historic Place Category 1. Constructed between the 1870s and the 1920s, the buildings were all designed to serve an educational purpose. Most housed the various departments and facilities of Canterbury College, the precursor of the University of Canterbury, which was founded in 1873, although two of the buildings were originally public high schools, one for girls and the other for boys. Over the half century of construction on the College's central city site, the institution and its architects stayed loyal to the foundational Gothic Revival style initiated by Benjamin Mountfort. The result is a remarkably coherent collection of buildings which expresses the Oxbridge educational aspirations of the Anglican Canterbury settlement. The rollcall of architects who worked at Canterbury College is a who's who of late nineteenth- and early twentieth-century Christchurch architecture: Mountfort, William Barnett Armson, Samuel Hurst Seager, John James Collins, Richard Dacre Harman. Only Cecil Wood didn't get a look in.

Heritage campaigners helped save the College buildings after the university moved to its new site in suburban Ilam in the 1960s and 1970s, and the campus has been converted into an arts and cultural venue. The buildings were damaged significantly in the 2010–2011 earthquakes; restoration has been extensive, expensive and impressive. Only a couple of buildings are yet to be rehabilitated. The regret that the university, and the central city, lost something through the Ilam diaspora has never quite gone away; lately, in a reverse migration, the university's music school and classics department have returned to the original campus (see Chemistry Laboratory, pages 26–27).

1   Christchurch Boys' High School
2   Clock Tower Block
3   Great Hall
4   Chemistry Laboratory
5   Canterbury College Library
6   Biology and Physics
7   Registry

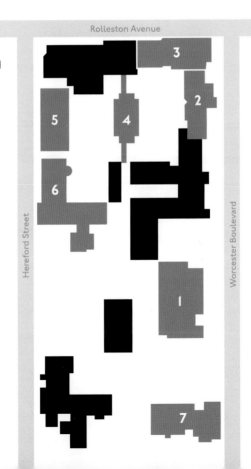

Great Hall (left) and West Lecture Building (Collins and Harman, 1917).
The Arts Centre Te Matatiki Toi Ora, facing Rolleston Avenue.

Christchurch Boys' High School

William Barnett Armson, 1881
Historic Place Category 1

Christchurch Boys' High School was founded a few years after, perhaps surprisingly, Christchurch Girls' High School. Like its sibling, it served as a feeder school to parent institution Canterbury College. The basalt and limestone Boys' High included teachers' rooms, a swimming pool, a fives court and the 'Big Room' used for assemblies and teaching. This room quickly gained a reputation for disorderly behaviour. The architecture, it seems, was to blame. In 1883, a government inspector opined that 'perhaps there was a little too much anxiety to produce an elegant building and too little care taken to make it thoroughly suitable for school pupils'.

This verdict would not have amused the building's architect, William Barnett Armson (1832/33–1883), if indeed he was still alive to read it. According to historian Jonathan Mane-Wheoki, Armson was a meticulous draughtsman who 'operated at a level of professionalism rare in New Zealand at that time', but the 'short, tubby and slightly bald' architect could be brusque with officials, clients and builders. Armson was born in England and raised in Melbourne; he came to Dunedin in 1862, and spent five years on the West Coast during the Gold Rush, designing banks, churches, hotels and Hokitika Town Hall (1866; no longer extant) before settling in Christchurch in 1870. Armson was prolific and stylistically fluent: many of his buildings were Italianate, but he had no trouble conforming to Canterbury College's Gothic Revival norm. Boys' High received several additions before outgrowing its site and moving from the Canterbury College campus in the mid-1920s. The building now houses shops and food outlets.

Clock Tower Block

Benjamin Mountfort, 1877
Historic Place Category 1

In the generation following the arrival of the Canterbury Association settlers in Christchurch in 1850, the colonists set about developing the institutions necessary to produce a facsimile of English society, minus an hereditary aristocracy at the top and a lumpenproletariat at the bottom. In quick order, the settlers built an Anglican church, founded a boys' school (Christ's College) and a hospital, laid the foundations for a cathedral (although, as in many places, cathedral completion was a Sisyphean task), and established provincial government. They also started newspapers, gentlemen's and cricket clubs, a horticulture society, and a museum. All this busyness, the colony's planners recognised, required some adjunct intellectual capacity. From the start, the Canterbury Association intended that education in the settlement would culminate in a tertiary level. In 1873, therefore, the Canterbury College board of governors announced a competition to design the College's buildings.

The competition was won by Benjamin Mountfort, and the first College building to be constructed was the Clock Tower Block. This building debuted the College's architectural genre — Gothic Revivalism, the house style of nineteenth-century High Anglicanism, and Mountfort's forte. If you wanted an emblematic Victorian building type, apart from the church, it would be hard to ignore the clock tower. The Canterbury College clock tower served the practical purpose of hastening students to their classes. It also sent a moral message: for the purposeful Victorians, time was a valuable resource, not to be wasted. The Clock Tower Block is now used as office accommodation, and also houses an exhibition space and café.

Great Hall

Benjamin Mountfort, 1882
Historic Place Category 1

The Great Hall was part of Benjamin Mountfort's competition-winning design for Canterbury College and it shows an architect at the height of his powers. By the time he designed the Great Hall, Mountfort had been in Christchurch for 30 years, having arrived as one of the original Canterbury Association settlers in 1850. He had received his architectural training, and ideological shaping, in London from Richard Cromwell Carpenter (1812–1855), a member of High Church Anglicanism's de facto architectural wing, the Ecclesiological Society. (The Society promoted the revival of both the religious ritual and Gothic architecture of the medieval church.) In Christchurch, Mountfort overcame an early setback — he made the rookie mistake of using unseasoned timber in a church in Lyttelton, which was built in 1853 and had to be demolished four years later — to become the leading architect of Canterbury Province.

Canterbury College Great Hall, constructed of basalt and limestone and lined on its barrel-vaulted interior with kauri, rewarewa, tōtara and matai, is a tour de force; it doesn't really matter that the original design's three towers were 'value managed' down to one. Mountfort's genius lies in his simultaneous adherence to the spirit of Gothic Revivalism and his relaxed observance of the rules of the genre. Note, for example, the arches above the windows of the Great Hall, which are segmented (gently curved) rather than lancet (pointed). The Great Hall retains a pointy Gothicness — the tower looks like a rocket about to be launched Godward — but also echoes a quality, 'not regularity of outline, but diversity', that Mountfort admired 'in Nature's buildings, the mountains and hills'. Building features such as the six bays of windows along the west face, the memorial window at the northern end, the stage at the southern end and the baronial fireplace, make the Great Hall one of New Zealand's most impressive rooms.

Chemistry Laboratory

Collins and Harman, 1910
Historic Place Category 1

This attractive building illustrates the accommodating nature of Gothic Revivalism when applied to an Oxbridge-inspired campus setting. The style could easily become less perpendicular and more horizontal — see, for example, Cecil Wood's historicist Hare Memorial Library at Christ College (pages 50–51) — to better frame lawns or quadrangles. At the Chemistry Laboratory a tower with an oriel window asymmetrically divides a triple-height arrangement of mullioned windows fitted between the building's buttresses; the tower has a turret, the end buttresses have finials, and the roof has a decorative ridge crest. A Gothic purist might find the design eclectic, but the pre-Modernist architects of the early twentieth century were not averse to stylistic promiscuity, often favouring compositional effect over consistency. With this building there is a strong sense of able architects delighting in the natural materials available to them in what was still a relatively young colony. The Chemistry Laboratory is, among other things, testament to the state of the regional quarrying industry in the early twentieth century: façade materials include Halswell, Hoon Hay and Tīmaru basalt, and Ōamaru limestone.

Architects John James Collins (1855–1933) and Richard Dacre Harman (1859–1927) had continued the firm started by William Barnett Armson (see pages 20–21) in 1870. Collins and Harman were busy through the 37 years of their partnership; their work included significant commercial projects such as the *Christchurch Press* Building (1909, demolished after the 2010–2011 earthquakes) and the still-extant Sign of the Takahe roadhouse (1936) in the Port Hills, as well as numerous gentry houses. The firm's work, and its reputation, was not confined to Christchurch and Canterbury; in Wellington, for example, the practice deployed the Gothic Revival style on the Dominion Farmers' Institute Building (1919).

Collins' and Harman's personal connections helped. Harman, in particular, got off to a flying, if competitive, start in life as one of

15 children of prominent businessman and politician Richard James Strachan Harman and his wife, Emma. Richard Harman senior had studied at Rugby School under the famous headmaster Thomas Arnold. Richard Harman junior enthusiastically played the game named for the English public (i.e., private) school but was better at tennis, his long run as Canterbury singles title-holder only ended by the future four-time Wimbledon champion and colonial golden boy Anthony Wilding (1883–1915).

The Chemistry Laboratory was restored after the 2010–2011 earthquakes by Warren and Mahoney Architects (2017), and the building is now occupied by the University of Canterbury's classics and music departments, back from their Ilam exile, and the Teece Museum of Classical Antiquities. The museum holds the James Logie Memorial Collection of Greek artefacts, established in 1957 by Marion Steven (1912–1999), a long-time lecturer in the university's classics department, and named by her in honour of her husband.

Chemistry Laboratory, The Arts Centre Te Matatiki Toi Ora.

Canterbury College Library (right), connected via an arcade to the West Lecture Building (left).

Canterbury College Library

Collins and Harman, 1916
Historic Place Category 1

In 1913, 40 years after Benjamin Mountfort started designing buildings on the Canterbury College campus, the College received an architectural reboot. Samuel Hurst Seager (1855–1933), a member of the College's board of governors and a lecturer in its School of Fine Arts, produced a new master plan for the campus with a view to more explicitly realising Mountfort's Oxbridge intentions. The principal instrument of this ambition was a College library. For Seager, the College's lack of a dedicated library was a serious omission. 'In any complete College, the Library is the centre of the Intellectual part of College Life,' Seager wrote. 'This should be architecturally expressed by its occupying a prominent central position.' The insertion into the heart of the campus of a library, joined to neighbouring buildings by arcades at its east and west ends, also served a planning purpose by creating separate Oxbridge-style quadrangles to the north and south of the building. The 1913 Student Carnival raised more than half of the £3500 cost of the building (less than $4 million in today's money, an impossibly inadequate figure for an equivalent contemporary building).

Although Seager had produced the master plan, the commission for the library's design went to Collins and Harman, the official Canterbury College architects from around the early 1900s until the late 1920s. The basalt and limestone library complements earlier buildings on the campus, although some Gothic–Tudor fusion is evident in the building's extensive glazing and arched windows. Restored post-earthquakes, the building now houses a dealer art gallery.

Biology and Physics

Benjamin Mountfort, 1896 (Biology, including Townsend Observatory); Collins and Harman, 1917 (Physics), 1918 (Biology extension)
Historic Place Category 1

The Physics and Biology buildings, the latter incorporating the wonderfully eccentric observatory, frame the south-east corner of the Arts Centre's South Quad. Biology — more properly the Biological Laboratory — came first. It was the last project at Canterbury College by Benjamin Mountfort, who died two years after its completion in 1896. Fun is not a quality automatically associated with Mountfort — Gothic Revivalism was a serious business — but he must have enjoyed designing the circular tower that is the Biology building's main feature. The tower was commissioned to house a 6-inch refracting telescope made by the English instrument manufacturer Thomas Cooke & Sons and donated to Canterbury College by early Christchurch settler and enthusiastic astronomer James Townsend (1815–1894), for whom it was named. Originally, the Townsend Observatory had a dome of wood and canvas; steel was used in the 1950 replacement. In the days when pranks were part of student life, the observatory's roof platform was an ideal launching pad for waterbombs lobbed into the quad.

The Biology building received an immediate neighbour when the Physics building with labs and lecture rooms was constructed in 1917, after a lobbying campaign supported by Canterbury College alumnus Ernest Rutherford, not yet the atom-splitter but already famous. Naturally, Collins and Harman employed the Gothic Revival style on the Physics building, and then on the extension connecting it with Biology. This was a tricky meeting; a corbelled turret, or tourelle, softens the abruptness of the right-angled join where the buildings intersect. The Biology and Physics buildings were badly damaged in the 2011 earthquake — the observatory tower was almost completely destroyed — but have been restored and now accommodate a boutique hotel. The Townsend telescope has also been restored and remains in the observatory dome.

Registry

Corner Montreal Street and Worcester Boulevard

Collins and Harman, 1916
Historic Place Category 1

In 1916–1917 there was a building boom on the campus of Canterbury College. It seems extraordinary that, in the middle of a world war, when every week newspapers were publishing poignant profiles of Canterbury soldiers killed or wounded in Belgium and France, the college could muster the physical and psychic resources to launch an ambitious construction programme. In short order, the campus received half a dozen new buildings — Library (pages 30–31), Common Room, Physics and Biology extension (pages 32–33), West Lecture and Registry. The latter was the bailiwick of the official who oversaw this rapid expansion, George Mason (1864–1934), Canterbury College registrar from 1908 to 1919. An efficient practitioner of the just-get-on-with-it school of institutional administration, Mason was also a sports bureaucrat, serving as president of the New Zealand Rugby Union and manager of the All Blacks on their 1913 tour of California.

Mason advocated for a separate building for Canterbury College's administrative staff, and was sufficiently powerful to realise his intention. The Registry building was commissioned from the College's architects, Collins and Harman, who produced a design compatible with Benjamin Mountfort's Gothic Revival campus precedents. Quoins and window frames are dressed up with creamy Ōamaru stone but, as historian Melanie Lovell-Smith notes, the relative paucity of decorative elements suggests a diminution in Gothic Revival fervour, perhaps owing to the building's prosaic purpose. Several extensions were added over the subsequent four decades. In the early 1970s, after Canterbury University had moved to Ilam, the building was threatened with demolition but was saved by a heritage campaign and preserved by its incorporation into the Arts Centre precinct. It was the first building in the Arts Centre to be restored after the 2010 and 2011 earthquakes, re-opening in 2013 to commercial occupation.

Ravenscar House Museum

52 Rolleston Avenue

Patterson Associates, 2021

With Ravenscar House Museum the shaky ground that brought so much of Christchurch down seems to have offered something back. The building looks like a crystalline eruption heaved up through the city's alluvial substrates. A pointy shape and pre-cast concrete walls salute Christchurch's Gothic and Brutalist traditions, but Ravenscar is an evolutionary jump in this design heredity, as well as a riposte to the post-quake orthodoxy of lighter-weight, steel-and-glass architecture. It's a strong, silent type, a chiselled object that reveals nothing of its interior life; the sheer planes of its walls — grey, relieved by flecks of red bricks recovered from quake rubble — give the building the formal singlemindedness of latest-generation stealth warships, no-frills machines with hulls resolved as seamless facets.

The building was designed by Patterson Associates, a firm on the radar of any client seeking a virtuoso design solution — commissions have included the Christchurch Botanic Gardens Visitor Centre (see pages 64–65) and New Plymouth's acclaimed Len Lye Centre (2015). Ravenscar House Museum is an idiosyncratic institution, both gallery and memorial, of time-honoured provenance. 'We all agree that we should endeavour to leave a reputation behind us,' observed the great quattrocento architectural dogmatist Leon Battista Alberti, 'for this reason, we erect great structures.' Ravenscar's full title positions it in the lineage of 'memory museums' — buildings holding their one-time owners' art and object collections — such as Sir John Soane's Museum in London. Operated by Canterbury Museum, Ravenscar houses New Zealand art, plus furniture and antiquities, collected by Susan and Jim Wakefield, the Christchurch business couple who commissioned the building, which is named for the Yorkshire village where Susan's family holidayed in her youth. Four rooms are connected by glazed links around a central pool. The design re-imagines the layout of the Wakefields' art-filled coastal Christchurch home, a casualty of the 2011 earthquake.

Christ's College

Rolleston Avenue

The buildings around Christ's College quad constitute one of
the strongest architectural compositions in New Zealand. The
site's distinction is not a matter of fortunate happenstance: it was
planned this way. From the start, the colonisers of Canterbury
envisaged that an integral institution of the settlement would be a
boys' school modelled on 'the great Grammar Schools of England'.
As time went by, the aspirations of the school became, if anything,
even grander, and Christ's took to taking its educational and cultural
lead from the great 'public' schools of England. Christ's College was
established on its present site adjacent to Hagley Park in 1856. Over
the course of more than a century and a half, wealth, tradition and
inter-generational fealty to the alma mater have found expression
in the commission, preservation and careful augmentation of fine
buildings by some of Christchurch's best architects, including the
Mountforts (father and son), John Collins and Richard Harman,
Cecil Wood, Paul Pascoe and Miles Warren.

9   Assembly Hall
10   Old Boys' Theatre
11   Jacobs House
12   School House
13   Hare Memorial Library
14   Big School
15   Chapel
16   Harper and Julius Houses
17   Memorial Dining Room

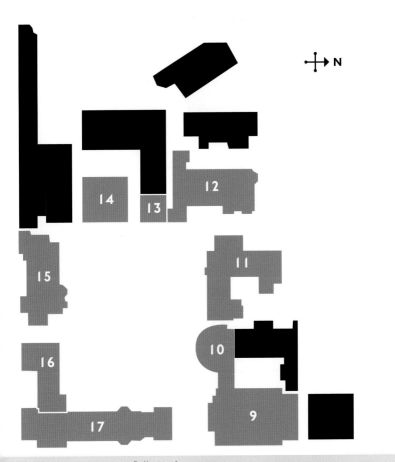

N

14

13

12

15

11

16

10

9

17

Rolleston Avenue

Gloucester Street

The Quadrangle at Christ's College.

Assembly Hall

Orchard and Allison, 1967
Historic Place Category 2

Christ's College Assembly Hall pairs with the Memorial Dining
Room (see pages 58–59) in forming the boundary between the
private realm of the school's quadrangle and the outside world on
Rolleston Avenue. As was usual, even at private schools, in the era
prior to the advent of secondary school performing arts centres,
the building had to earn its keep by accommodating a variety
of occasions and events: school assemblies, exams and prize-
givings, theatrical productions, choral performances and gymnastic
competitions. In the 1970s, writes Miles Warren, movies would
be screened in the hall on Saturday nights to keep the boarders
happy (an outcome contingent on the competence of the student
projectionist). The hall, which could seat up to 1000 people, was
renowned for its acoustic qualities and, at the time of its opening,
the standard of its lighting and sound equipment and heating and
ventilation systems.

The commission was won in a design competition, limited
to old boys of Christ's College, by the Auckland-based practice
headed by Neil Orchard (1907–1983) and David Allison (1923–
2010), the latter a Christ's alumnus. Orchard and Allison was one
of the numerous competent, if not celebrated, Modernist practices
working throughout New Zealand from the late 1950s to the end of
the 1970s. There's something to be said for the ubiquity of a style
with readily understood principles, and in many of the country's
towns buildings surviving from those Modernist decades put their
younger neighbours to architectural shame. In the rhythms of its
progress along Rolleston Avenue, and the deployment on its lower
level of grey stone cladding, the Assembly Hall echoes the stately
march of Cecil Wood's Memorial Dining Room. Orchard and Allison
played a simpler and sprightlier tune, though, re-imagining Wood's
chunky buttresses as slim concrete fins that divide sections of tall
windows into shallow and elegant bays.

Old Boys' Theatre

Miles Warren, 2000

Successful architects know which client buttons to push. Beyond responding to the requirements of a brief, they give clients the understanding they want and the reassurance they need. Among the many talents of Miles Warren (1929–2022), Christchurch's outstanding later-twentieth-century architect, was his ability to provide a convincing rationale, or compelling narrative, to accompany a design concept. The Old Boys' Theatre at Christ's College was a case in point — a project that demanded Warren reconcile amenity with context while allaying some institutional nervousness. For Warren, then retired from Warren and Mahoney, the theatre was the latest in a series of commissions from his old school and 'most rewarding client' stretching back to 1959, when he designed a lavatory block for the college, a structure he later described, sounding just like young Warren minor, the scholarship boy, as 'an eight-holer, basic concrete, no doors on the bogs'.

Warren was able to tether the design of a 200-seat theatre to an upgrade of Richards House (Helmore and Cotterill, 1956), a building set back awkwardly from the quad. In the latter stages of a career grounded in the geometrics of Modernism, Warren proved susceptible to the attractions of post-Modern curvilinearity. (The inclination was probably always there, thanks to all those Beaux-Arts-style drawing assignments in the 1940s Christchurch 'atelier'.) The Salvation Army Citadel in Wellington (1984) and Saint Patrick's Church, Napier (1990), were semi-circular precedents for the Old Boys' Theatre, which pushes into Christ's quadrangle. Warren justified the projection — somewhat dubiously, he admitted — by arguing that although the curve extends past Jacobs House (pages 46–47) it recedes at its south end so, on average, lines up with its neighbour. The theatre is faced in basalt from the demolished St Mary's Convent (see pages 168–69); the upper-level windows are framed in Ōamaru stone, as homage to Jacobs House and its architect, Cecil Wood.

Jacobs House

Cecil Wood, 1930
Historic Place Category 2

Named for the first headmaster of Christ's College, Reverend
Henry Jacobs (1824–1901), this boarding house on the north side
of the quad was designed by Cecil Wood (1878–1947), one of the
foremost New Zealand architects of the first half of the twentieth
century. It was Wood's third building on the college campus and
was designed in formal and material sympathy to existing buildings
on the quad, especially the neighbouring School House. On the
side facing the quad, the building is styled as an historicist blend
of Gothic Revival and Collegiate Gothic, with an admixture of
Georgian Revival to boot. This façade of the L-shaped, slate-roofed
building is made of Hoon Hay rubble stone, relieved by the use of
white Ōamaru stone on the entranceway, window surrounds and
a string course, and Redcliffs volcanic stone on the battlements.
At the rear, the building is plainer, and presents an overtly neo-
Georgian brick face to the Ōtākaro Avon River.

   The string course on the quad façade is decorated with seven
stone heads by carver Frederick George Gurnsey (1868–1953).
Welsh-born Gurnsey studied ecclesiastical carving in Exeter, ran
an antique shop in Glastonbury, visited New Zealand for health
reasons in 1904–1905, and immigrated to Christchurch two years
later to teach at the Canterbury College of Art. From 1923 he was
a full-time carver, completing hundreds of commissions around
the country. Gurnsey's Christchurch work includes carvings at
the Bridge of Remembrance (see pages 88–89), the Church of
St Michael and All Angels (see pages 86–87) and the Public Trust
Office Building (see pages 94–95).

School House

Cyril Mountfort; Armson, Collins and Harman, 1909
Historic Place Category 2

School House is a Collegiate Gothic building for boarders designed by Cyril Julian Mountfort (1852–1920), and John Collins and Richard Harman. The main façade is constructed of local Halswell stone, with window arches in white Ōamaru stone, and features a small cloister. On its other, less visible, sides the building is brick. An observatory, designed by Cecil Wood, was added to the roof in 1936. (Star-gazing is a venerable tradition in Christchurch — see also Benjamin Mountfort's observatory at Canterbury College, pages 32–33).

Architecturally, School House could be seen as an act of filial piety; it is similar to the building that sits diagonally across the quad — Harper and Julius Houses (1886), designed by Cyril Mountfort's father, Benjamin. Cyril Mountfort's career was overshadowed by his eminent father, although he oversaw the completion of ChristChurch Cathedral (see pages 136–37) and designed a number of churches, mainly around Christchurch, in the Gothic Revival style.

John Collins and Richard Harman were far more successful. Inheritors of the practice established by William Barnett Armson, Collins and Harman worked in partnership for nearly four decades. (The firm itself lasted for 123 years.) Like Cyril Mountfort, Collins and Harman were old boys of Christ's College, and very clubbable, and their social connections provided a steady stream of residential commissions from pastoral landowners and urban professionals. The story of Collins and Harman's progress is also a narrative of the changes in sensibility of an essentially conservative clientele, as local architectural tastes evolved from Gothic and Tudor Revival to Arts and Crafts and eventually modern bungalow.

Hare Memorial Library

Cecil Wood, 1915
Historic Place Category 1

With the design of Hare Memorial Library, Cecil Wood went a little wild — kind of Hogwarts wild. The library, which was named for Francis Augustus Hare (1845–1912), a Christ's College chaplain and headmaster, was the first of Wood's three buildings around the quad. Wood (1878–1947) was an exception to Christ's custom of engaging its old boys as architects. He was educated privately at Miss Leete's School and publicly at West Christchurch School before his engineer father paid architect Frederick Strouts (see pages 78–79) £100 to take him on as an 'articled' employee. (This form of apprenticeship was a traditional way — for young males — into the architecture profession.) He worked for Clarkson and Ballantyne (see pages 110–11) and attended evening classes at Canterbury College, where he was taught by Samuel Hurst Seager (see pages 30–31), before spending five years in England. Although his uncle Norman Shaw (1831–1912) was a leading British architect, Wood made his own way in the UK where he spent some time working for London County Council on the design of what we would now call social housing.

At the Hare Memorial Library, Wood demonstrated appropriate deference to Gothic Revival precedent, but introduced Tudor twists in the form of an oriel window, arched gateway and thin chimneys. (The Gothic gargoyles carved by Frederick Gurnsey look as if they have been captured in mid-leap from the building's stylistic apostasy.) The variegated colour palette of the façade — grey Malvern stone, red Sumner volcanic stone and cream Mount Somers limestone — combine with Wood's antiquarian references to produce what is almost a parodically picturesque building. It is extraordinary to think, if you allow yourself to zoom out of the quad, spatially and temporally, that in 10 years' time Walter Gropius would be designing the Bauhaus building in Dessau.

Big School

James Edward FitzGerald, 1863;
addition by Miles Warren, 1989
Historic Place Category 1

Big School was the first substantial building on the Christ's College campus. It was designed in England, with an eye to pedagogical tradition but little geographical awareness — hence the roof steeply pitched to counter alpine snowfalls — by James Edward FitzGerald (1818–1896), a typically energetic Victorian genre-buster.

FitzGerald started out as a junior in the Antiquities Department of the British Museum, found quick promotion and, on the side, involved himself in social and political causes. As Secretary of the Canterbury Association he helped plan the Canterbury settlement and decided to immigrate to it, in short order serving as a police officer, newspaper publisher and farm owner. FitzGerald was elected superintendent of Canterbury Province and was later a member of Parliament with comparatively enlightened views on race relations. He became a Wellington senior civil servant before heading a trade union for civil servants. In his spare time, FitzGerald painted watercolours and wrote verse and drama; his wife, Frances, presumably took primary responsibility for the couple's 13 children.

Big School, a rectangular structure with stone walls, slate roof, timber ceiling and leaded windows, seems to have been the only building FitzGerald designed. He appears to have been unfazed by his complete lack of architectural training, and confident in his blunt ideological purpose. The building, FitzGerald said, was intended to impress upon its young occupants the qualities of 'massive strength, stability, and simplicity of character'. In 1989, Big School received an addition of five gabled wings, designed by an indubitably proper architect, Miles Warren. It may be the oldest educational building in Aotearoa New Zealand in continuous use.

Chapel

Robert Speechly, 1867; additions by Benjamin Mountfort (1883, 1887) and Paul Pascoe (1957)
Historic Place Category 1

Christ's College Chapel was designed by Robert Speechly (1840–1884), who was sent from England to Canterbury by the great Gothic Revival architect George Gilbert Scott, senior (1811–1878), to supervise the construction of ChristChurch Cathedral (see pages 136–37) and function, effectively, as the Church of England's local architect-in-residence. Speechly, controversially, was bumped from the cathedral project in favour of Benjamin Mountfort, but stayed in Christchurch for four years, designing several churches and vicarages. Gothic Revivalism was the architectural language of the mid-nineteenth-century Anglican Church, and Speechly adopted the style for Christ College's chapel, a modest stone building that materially, and in the form of its steep slate roof, complemented the existing Big School. Benjamin Mountfort added transepts and a chancel (1883) and organ chamber (1887) to the chapel, and that was it until Paul Pascoe (1908–1976) designed a sympathetic extension to the south that doubled the building's size.

Pascoe was a Christ's College old boy who trained with Cecil Wood before a sojourn in England in the mid-1930s confirmed his Modernist inclinations. (When it came to choosing its post-war architects, Christ's evidently did not let its traditionalism blind it to design ability, provided competence was allied with alumnus status.) Pascoe was a highly regarded designer, especially of houses and churches; airport architecture was another of his specialties. He was a student of comparative religion and a keen tramper and mountain climber — his twin John (d.1972) was a leading New Zealand alpinist and mountaineering writer — and, naturally enough, he volunteered to design the landmark chapel at Arthur's Pass (1956). After a decade in a productive partnership with Humphrey Hall (1912–1988), Pascoe was a sole practitioner at the time he designed the extension to Christ's College Chapel.

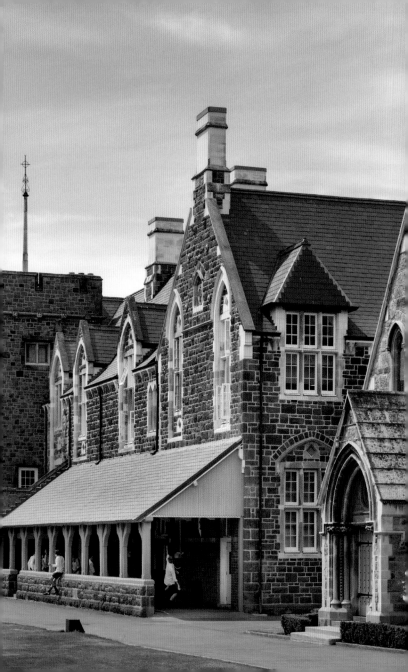

Harper and Julius Houses

Benjamin Mountfort, 1886

Christ's College caters for both boarders and 'dayboys', and organises both categories of student into 'houses'. Harper and Julius Houses are dayboy houses, formerly called South Town and North Town — membership was determined by students' addresses in the city — that for nearly a century have occupied what was originally a classroom block, designed by Benjamin Mountfort, on the south side of the quad. Harper House was the first house assigned to the Gothic Revival building; the bottom floor was converted to accommodate Julius House in 1931. Further renovations were undertaken in 1962 and 1981. After the building was damaged in the 2010–2011 earthquakes, it was seismically strengthened, and the exterior was restored under the supervision of Wilkie + Bruce Architects (2013). The Gothicness of the interior had been significantly compromised by the earlier alteration work.

Christ's College is not short of atmospheric places that must imprint themselves forever in the memory of those who study there, but even amidst this evocative abundance the cloister — a neo-Gothic lean-to — of the Harper and Julius building is special. It is the sort of space boys love, an open-air den. On the day Patrick Reynolds took the photo at left, the cloister was in cricket wicket mode, its open end allowing a decent run-up, but right through the year it must be one of the best places on the quad to just hang out. The cloister has a sibling diagonally across the quad — School House, co-designed by Benjamin Mountfort's son, Cyril.

Memorial Dining Room

Cecil Wood, 1925
Historic Place Category 1

Christchurch is fortunate to have, less than 200 metres apart, two of the finest large rooms in Aotearoa New Zealand: the Canterbury College Great Hall (see pages 24 –25) and Christ's College Memorial Dining Room. The Christ's College building is probably, and deservedly, the most acclaimed work of Cecil Wood. It memorialises old boys of the school who served in the First World War — more than 130 lost their lives — and does so without stint: the Dining Room cost twice as much as the city's Bridge of Remembrance (see pages 88–89). Wood deployed the Collegiate Gothic style — species to the Gothic Revival genus — on a building that defines the east side of the quad and presents a public face to Rolleston Avenue. The building features a square tower where it meets Benjamin Mountfort's 1886 classroom block (Harper and Julius Houses), half a dozen buttresses on the east and west sides, oriel bay windows and a façade composed of grey Hoon Hay rubble, Redcliffs volcanic stone and Ōamaru limestone.

Inside, Wood got medieval; historian Ruth Helms has pointed out the Dining Room's links to the manorial Great Hall at the Oxford college Christ Church, especially in the use of timber linenfold panelling — timber carved in vertical folds — and ribbed hammerbeam Oregon roof trusses, their ends decorated with winged figures carved by Frederick Gurnsey. Ōamaru stone lines the upper portion of the hall's interior. At the south end of the hall, which can accommodate 350 diners, is a raised dais; at the north end, a musicians' gallery.

Wood was commissioned in the 1940s to design an extension at the northern end of the building, but a funding shortage halted the project. The addition, housing school offices, was completed in 1988 to a design by Miles Warren.

Canterbury Museum

Rolleston Avenue at Worcester Boulevard

Benjamin Mountfort, 1870–1882
Historic Place Category I

Canterbury Museum is a monument to two of New Zealand's eminent Victorians, and to the collecting mania of their age. Institutionally, the museum owes a debt to its inaugural director, Julius von Haast (1822–1987); architecturally, the credit belongs to Benjamin Mountfort. Haast, an ambitious Prussian geology graduate, was commissioned in 1858 by an English shipping company to travel to New Zealand and report on the prospects for German emigration. His arrival was coincident with that of Austrian geologist Ferdinand von Hochstetter (1829–1884). Haast helped Hochstetter undertake the first geological survey of New Zealand and then pursued a career as a mapper, prospecting geologist and scientific explorer. He was an avid collector of geological and zoological specimens; in the mid-1860s, he alighted on some spectacular discoveries — moa bones, which he trafficked to European museums, and a skeleton of the extinct *Hieraaetus moorei*, or Haast's eagle. (Possessed of a considerable ego, Haast would have been gratified that his name was attached to the world's largest raptor.)

In 1861 Haast established his own museum in Christchurch and then advocated successfully for a public museum. A design competition yielded two winning entries, those of Robert Speechly and Benjamin Mountfort, before the Provincial Government awarded the commission to the Provincial Engineer, Edward Dobson (1816/17–1908), who was Haast's father-in-law. Mountfort re-captured the commission, designing a stone building (1870) and, over the next dozen years, three extensions, all generally cleaving to the architect's signature Gothic Revival style. The museum was further extended in 1958 and 1977, and seismically strengthened. In the early 2000s, a renovation scheme devised by Athfield Architects and defended by Miles Warren was stymied by heritage resisters, led by Peter Beaven. The building survived the 2010–2011 earthquakes in good shape.

Robert McDougall Art Gallery

9 Rolleston Avenue, Botanic Gardens

Edward Armstrong, 1932
Historic Place Category 1

The Robert McDougall Art Gallery served as Christchurch's public art gallery for 70 years until its spatial and functional limitations saw it replaced by a much larger modern building (see pages 70–71). Early on, it struggled to find the love, despite the conventional charm of its appearance and its philanthropic provenance, but became a cherished civic institution. The gallery was built to house the art collection gifted to the city in 1925 by local construction contractor James Jamieson (1842–1927) on the condition that it be housed in a new building. In a referendum, the public voted against the council taking out a loan to finance a building, but in 1928 Robert McDougall (1860–1942), owner of Aulsebrooks & Co. — the largest biscuit-maker in Australasia — donated £25,000, later topped up to £31,000, for a new gallery.

The gallery design competition was won by Edward Armstrong (1896–1992), the architect son of Gisborne's city engineer. When he entered the competition, Armstrong, who had won a scholarship to the British School in Rome and then worked for several years in Burma, was based in England, where he was to stay until returning to Gisborne in the 1950s. Armstrong's neo-Classical building, made of concrete and brick relieved by Ōamaru stone, centres, on the exterior, on a portico, and, in the interior, a lofty central hall with a marble floor and columns rendered in scagliola, a marble-looking plaster composite. Natural light is admitted into the gallery via skylights, following the example of Samuel Hurst Seagar's Sarjeant Gallery in Whanganui (1919). The council's allocated site for the gallery — in the Botanic Gardens, barely, and abutting the backside of Canterbury Museum — handicapped its visual appeal. The building survived the 2010–2011 earthquakes; now, as melancholy as a mausoleum, it awaits restoration and, possibly and controversially, absorption into Canterbury Museum.

Christchurch Botanic Gardens Visitor Centre

Patterson Associates, 2014

The most fortunate legacy of Christchurch's gestation as a planned settlement is the extensive reserve on the west side of the central city. Most of this greenbelt — 185 hectares — is given over to the woodland and playing fields of Hagley Park, but since 1863 another 21 hectares, circumscribed by a loop of the Avon River, have been occupied by the Christchurch Botanic Gardens. The Gardens have numerous formal planted areas, including the New Zealand Gardens, a pinetum rosarium, Asian collection and water garden. Half a dozen conservatories (including Cuningham House, see pages 66–67) were built in the Gardens in the twentieth century; in 2014, they were joined by the Visitor Centre designed by Patterson Associates.

The Visitor Centre, which includes a café, shop, library, exhibition space and plant propagation areas, was one of the city's first earthquake recovery projects. The granting of such a notable Christchurch civic commission to an Auckland-based architecture practice was perhaps surprising — in architecture, as with other pursuits, Canterbury has a tradition, often justified, of provincial preference — but the outcome justified the adventure. (Patterson Associates was soon awarded another prestigious Christchurch commission: Ravenscar House Museum, see pages 36–37.)

In their design of the Botanic Gardens Visitor Centre, Patterson Associates celebrated a traditional garden building type. The Visitor Centre is adapted from a Dutch commercial greenhouse construction system; it proceeds along its site in a rhythmic march of modular units and saw-tooth roofs. Inside, the building is also white but not quite as bright. Natural light is filtered through fritted glass and plays upon the patterned concrete of interior walls and ceilings.

Cuningham House

Botanic Gardens

Collins and Harman, 1924
Historic Place Category 2

The orangery housing exotic fruit trees was an aristocratic indulgence in northern Europe from the seventeenth to nineteenth centuries, but Joseph Paxton's Crystal Palace at London's 1851 Great Exhibition launched the Winter Garden as a popular attraction. The large, boiler-heated, extensively glazed conservatories of Victorian Britain were showcases for the botanical spoils of conquest — flora from the warmer regions of an empire on which the sun never set. Eventually, the building type reached the farthest-flung colony. Dunedin got its Winter Garden glasshouse in 1908 and the Temperate House in Auckland Domain opened in 1921. Christchurch caught up in 1924 thanks to a bequest from Charles Cuningham (1850–1915), an Irish child immigrant who, from the age of 12, clerked in Christchurch law offices. A keen gardener and regular visitor to the Botanic Gardens, Cuningham was a much-respected citizen — 'most unostentatious', noted an obituarist for *The Star*, but hardly a stick-in-the-mud, 'having seen 74 countries and islands in his time'.

When designing the new display house, architects Collins and Harman looked to the Winter Gardens in Springburn Park, Glasgow, a site familiar to the Botanic Gardens' long-time curator, or head gardener, Scots-born James Young (1862–1934), and Domain board member James Jamieson (see pages 62–63). Neo-Classical Cuningham House is symmetrically arranged around a south-facing portico, with Tuscan columns and a balustraded terrace, axially aligned with the adjacent Rose Garden. Inside, a central double-height exhibition area — the municipal glasshouse being to plants what the public gallery is to art — is overlooked by a mezzanine and topped with a domed roof supported by steel trusses and capped by a glazed lantern. Altered, but not significantly, last century, and repaired after the 2010–2011 earthquakes, Cuningham House endures as the Botanic Gardens' most impressive built feature.

ROUTE 2:
RIVER SIDE

This part of the central city, one-block deep on either side of the Ōtākaro Avon River, contains many important cultural and institutional buildings, including the city's art gallery and Benjamin Mountfort's Provincial Government Building. There are fine examples of concrete Modernism, among them CoCA Gallery and the office and townhouse designed by Miles Warren, the leading Christchurch architect of his generation. Two very different memorial sites are located on the route: one commemorates those who fell in the First World War, the other those who died in the earthquake of 22 February 2011. On the east bank of the river, The Terrace has been restored as a lively hospitality strip.

Christchurch Art Gallery
Te Puna o Waiwhetū

Corner Worcester Boulevard and Montreal Street

The Buchan Group, 2003

In 1998, Christchurch City Council staged a design competition for a public art gallery to replace the Robert McDougall Art Gallery (see pages 62–63) located in the Botanic Gardens. The new building was to occupy a new site, close to the city's two strongest collections of heritage buildings, the Arts Centre and Christ's College. (That was a lot of precedence to respond to, resist, or ignore.) To some local surprise, the competition, which attracted 94 entries, was won by the Auckland office of a practice of Australian origin, The Buchan Group.

   The competition judges were impressed by the most obvious feature of the design, the glass façade on the west elevation. With its 'association with the curved shapes of the Koru and to the serpentine course of the Avon River,' the judges said, the glazed wall expresses 'the public face of the building, its identity as an Art Gallery.' The latter remark was revealing: an exciting form had come to be regarded as an essential quality of the art museum. The Guggenheim had worked its effect, first in New York (Frank Lloyd Wright, 1959) and then, even more influentially, in Bilbao (Frank Gehry, 1997). However, the glass wall is not just a signifier; it serves to connect the building to an extensive sculpture garden and admits light into the three-storey lobby that fronts the traditional box-shaped rooms in which the gallery's collections are exhibited.

   In the aftermath of the 2011 earthquake, the art gallery was used as the Emergency Operating Centre for the recovery effort. It was then closed for extensive repairs, including the retro-fitting of 140 base isolators, before re-opening in late 2015.

Toi Moroki Centre of Contemporary Art (CoCA) Gallery

66 Gloucester Street

Minson, Henning-Hansen and Dines, 1968

It's not easy to appreciate, from the perspective of the present, how radical some buildings from the past must have appeared when they were new. Take, for example, Toi Moroki Centre of Contemporary Art (CoCA) Gallery. Built by what was then the Canterbury Society of Arts to replace its former premises — two late nineteenth-century brick buildings on another site, one of them designed by, yes, Benjamin Mountfort — CoCA introduced itself to its heritage neighbourhood with uncompromising severity. Even in a city softened up to concrete Modernism by a decade of Miles Warren Brutalism, the building, with its façade of twin aggregate slabs, must have come as a shock.

How did it happen? Because the client was a private entity, and therefore not subject to the committee caution that can cripple public projects, and because the panel that wrote the brief included three architects — Miles Warren, Peter Beaven and Paul Pascoe. And, especially, because the commission went to one of the able Modernist practices that characterised Christchurch architecture in the 1960s, the partnership of Stewart William Minson (1904–2006), Holger Henning-Hansen (1921–1996) and John Rayner Dines (1927–1993). This fine little building seems particularly congruent with the Scandinavian Modernist inclinations of Danish immigrant Henning-Hansen. If you look up, it is possible to discern, in CoCA's rooftop cluster of pyramidal skylights, a reference to the Christchurch tradition of pointy architecture.

151 Cambridge Terrace

Jasmax, 2014

While the 2011 Christchurch earthquake was immediately frightening, for people who grew up in the city the long-running aftermath has been profoundly disorienting. As hundreds of damaged or vulnerable buildings — or those so deemed — were demolished all around the CBD, the concept of place was also dismantled. In parts of the central city, there was no 'there' there anymore. Which brings us to the subject of context in architecture: when architects discuss the factors that have influenced their designs, they habitually invoke the notion of 'context'. The reference may be meaningful or moonshine; it can allude to neighbouring buildings or the wider city, to local architectural history or an indigenous building type, to cultural tropes or features of the natural world.

The latter well of inspiration was the one visited by Jasmax when designing this large commercial building on a prominent site next to the west bank of the Ōtākaro Avon River. Absent any other contextual clues in what had become a demolition zone, the architects turned to the river itself and echoed its winding course in the aqua-coloured sections of the new building's glass façade. The building was an early indicator of a generic shift in post-quake Christchurch from masonry buildings — heavy but seismically weak — to more resilient, often extensively glazed structures of sudden contemporaneity. 151 Cambridge Terrace is base isolated on pendulum bearings, a construction technology that, it is claimed, will let the building ride out an earthquake by allowing it to move as much as 500 millimetres in any direction.

Worcester Chambers

69 Worcester Boulevard

Cecil Wood, 1928
Historic Place Category 2

Looking at old buildings can be like reading old novels. The florid
expressions and rhetorical flourishes that characterised pre-
Modernist literature have their equivalents in pre-Modernist
architecture, and the diet can be too rich for contemporary
taste. But one historical style that is easier to digest is Georgian
architecture, which valued order, proportion and a certain material
frugality above flamboyant forms and box-of-tricks ornamentation.
The Georgian style enjoyed a revival in Anglo-Saxon countries in
the early twentieth century and in Christchurch was championed by
Cecil Wood.

The building now known as Worcester Chambers is a well-
mannered example of Wood's Georgian Revival phase. Designed
to house the Digby family's commercial school (curriculum:
shorthand, typing, book-keeping, commercial practice and business
correspondence), the brick building has a hipped slate roof with
two cornice-topping urns, symmetrically arranged double-hung
sash windows with keystones, a hood supported by corbels above
the front door, cement quoins framing the street elevation and a
scalloped cement band at footpath level. All in all, a nice piece of
streetscape, which deserves some tender ministration.

Wood probably could have designed this building in his sleep,
not that he would have, being by all accounts a person of much
integrity. Historian Ruth Helms suggests he deserves a place in
the front rank of New Zealand inter-war architecture alongside
Auckland's W. H. Gummer (1884–1966), and Wellington's William
Gray Young (1895–1962). In his later career, Wood's traditionalist
inclinations attracted some Modernist disdain — his 1937
commission for Wellington's Anglican Cathedral of St Paul's may
have been a late-career bridge too far — even if his talent continued
to be acknowledged.

Canterbury Club

129 Cambridge Terrace

Frederick Strouts, 1874
Historic Place Category 2

A reprise in newly established Christchurch of the venerable British schism between the rural gentry and the urban bourgeoisie gave birth in 1872 to the Canterbury Club. Members of the settlement's business and professional classes evidently had felt unwelcome or uncomfortable in the Christchurch Club, which had been founded in 1856 as a home-away-from-the-farm for country 'runholders' (see pages 152–53). Having founded their own club, the arrivistes — how rapid was the colonial recrudescence of metropolitan social stratification — ordered a building from one of their own, architect William Armson. When Armson fell ill, the Club turned to Frederick Strouts (1834–1919), a Kentish-born architect who had arrived in Canterbury in 1859 and co-founded a typically catch-all settler enterprise which advertised itself as 'General Importers & Ironmongers, Architects, Surveyors & Land Agents'. Increasingly, Strouts focused on practising architecture and raising the profession's standing; in 1876, he won a court case that gave architects the right to retain plans for unbuilt commissions.

For the Canterbury Club, Strouts adopted the Italianate style that Benjamin Mountfort — himself following London clubland precedent — had deployed, more coherently, on the Christchurch Club. Strouts' design incorporated a two-storey wing on the corner of Cambridge Terrace and Worcester Boulevard and a single-storey wing on Worcester Boulevard that was extended in 1907 by Armson, Collins and Harman. (After Armson's death in 1883, his younger partners retained his name in the firm's title for many years.) Two adjacent street features have their own Historic Place Category 2 classification: the sole survivor (c1875) of the gas lamps that once lit Christchurch's streets — there were more than 1300 in 1913, just prior to the city's electrification — and a hitching post installed by the Canterbury Club around the late 1870s to 1880s, a time when both town and country gentlemen travelled by horse.

Te Pou
Herenga Waka

Te Hononga Christchurch Civic Building

53 Hereford Street

Government Architect's Office, MoW, 1981
Athfield Architects, 2010

Te Hononga Christchurch Civic Building impressively represents several phenomena of both architectural and social significance. It is a case study in sustainability and — literally — a monument to the role of the state as architect and builder in New Zealand and to the historic importance of the post office in the socio-economic life of the country.

The building was designed as a mail sorting facility by the Architectural Division (headed by the Government Architect) of the Ministry of Works and Development (MoW). It started its project life in 1965, but MoW jobs had a long lead time and the building was not completed until 1981. The grunty industrial building expressed the MoW's Brutalist tendencies of the 1960s and 1970s and a concomitant partiality for reinforced concrete as a construction medium. (In an era of import restrictions, concrete offered the advantage of high local content.)

The post office's enfeeblement after the economic deregulation of the late 1980s eventually robbed the building of its purpose, and in the first decade of this century it was converted by Athfield Architects into the headquarters of Christchurch City Council. The energy embodied in the building's construction has not been wasted, nor has the structure been much changed. Concrete façade panels were replaced with glass to admit light into the building's seven 5.8-metre-high floors, and a ground-level walkway now connects Te Hononga's two entrances, one on Hereford Street and the other on Worcester Boulevard.

65 Cambridge Terrace

Warren and Mahoney, 1962 (with additions up to 1989)

In 1955, Miles Warren returned to Christchurch after two years in England experiencing, as an architect for London County Council, the heyday of British municipal Modernism and springtime of New Brutalism. Back home, he launched a practice which was soon joined by Maurice Mahoney (1929–2018) — for 35 years, Dr Watson to Warren's Sherlock Holmes — and embarked on one of the hottest streaks in New Zealand architecture. For a decade and a half, the hits kept coming: Dorset Street Flats (1957, see pages 174–75), Harewood Crematorium Chapel (1963), College House (1964, see pages 185–89), Christchurch College Chapel and Library (1967–1970), and Christchurch Town Hall (1972, see pages 164–67).

Even among its peers, 65 Cambridge Terrace is an outstanding building. Sited in what was then a residential zone, the building was cannily conceived as both a practice office for Warren and Mahoney and a regulation-satisfying house. (Local zoning meant at least half of the building had to have a residential use.) It is a miniaturist masterpiece, real architect's architecture, but also a builder's building. 'Miles made a great play of how he put his buildings together,' wrote architect and critic David Mitchell, 'articulating every joint, which is a fabricator's way of looking at architecture.'

At 65 Cambridge Terrace Warren was showing off, treating the town to a Brutalist exposition of concrete beams and blocks, but also exhibiting a deft command of details and a typically impish capacity to delight. Over the years, as the office grew and the neighbourhood was re-classified as a commercial zone, the building was altered and extended. An L-shaped flat was pushed into the rear walled garden; Warren's other great love was to receive grander expression in the formal gardens at Ōhinetahi, his home at Governors Bay, near Lyttelton.

Oi Manawa Canterbury Earthquake National Memorial

Ōtākaro Avon River at Montreal Street and Oxford Street

Grega Vezjak, 2017

Oi Manawa Canterbury Earthquake National Memorial opened on 22 February 2017, the sixth anniversary of the earthquake that killed 185 people in Christchurch. The memorial encompasses both banks on a curve of the Ōtākaro Avon River downstream from the Montreal Street bridge. Along the south bank of the hectare-sized site, a riverside walkway leads past a 111-metre-long, 3.6-metre-high Carrara marble wall bearing the names of those who lost their lives; the north bank is an informal reserve that offers contemplative views across the river to the memorial wall.

The memorial is the result of a design competition that attracted 339 entries from around the world and was won by Slovenian architect Grega Vezjak. Not surprisingly, Vezjak's design has some affinity with the most influential memorial of the past half-century, Maya Lin's Vietnam Veterans Memorial (1982) in Washington DC. Where Lin's memorial wall is partially buried in the earth, Vezjak's wall sinks below street level to connect with the Ōtākaro Avon River. The design of both memorials encourages visitors to search for and touch the names inscribed into the stone walls.

Oi Manawa — the Māori term translates in English as 'the tremor or quivering of the heart' — is the sort of memorial that bereaved families indicated they wanted: not an object or a ruin, but a place, close to nature. A visit to W. H. Gummer's memorial arch at the Bridge of Remembrance (1924), a short distance away (see pages 88–89), serves to show how far official remembering has come in the last hundred years.

Church of St Michael and All Angels, and Belfry

84 Oxford Terrace

William Fitzjohn Crisp, 1872 (church)
Benjamin Mountfort, 1861 (belfry)
Historic Place Category 1

In 1851, the Anglican settlers of Christchurch built the first
church on the Canterbury Plains, initially called Christ Church,
then re-named St Michael and All Angels. The congregation soon
outgrew the church and commissioned a replacement on the same
site from William Fitzjohn Crisp (1846–1924), a young English
immigrant architect. Crisp designed the building in the Gothic
Revival style popular in British ecclesiastical architecture. There
was one significant concession to local circumstances: a meeting
of the parishioners, reported Christchurch newspaper *The Star* in
December 1869, concluded that 'owing to the late severe shocks
of earthquake . . . it would be useless to attempt building any part
of stone. Therefore it was decided that wood should be the
material.' Mataī was the native timber chosen for the structure,
supported by a rubble stone foundation. The combination of
dark wood and English stained glass windows makes for a richly
atmospheric interior.

The relationship between the congregation and their architect
broke down during construction and Crisp returned to Britain in
1871. Frederick Strouts (see pages 78–79) was appointed in his
place. The church never received its planned bell tower and spire
but is kept company by the free-standing belfry designed by
the ubiquitous Benjamin Mountfort. Christchurch architectural
historian Ian Lochhead suggests the belfry's canopy was inspired
by the famous Saxon-type tower of St Mary the Blessed Virgin,
a thousand-year-old church — once the property of the Knights
Templar — in the West Sussex village of Sompting.

Bridge of Remembrance

Ōtākaro Avon River at Cashel Street

Gummer and Prouse, 1924
Historic Place Category 1

In the years after the First World War, in which around 18,000 New Zealanders lost their lives, hundreds of memorials were erected around the country. Memorial architecture included statues, obelisks, towers, gates and even entire buildings, such as Auckland's War Memorial Museum Tāmaki Paenga Hira. The Bridge of Remembrance is one of the two main Christchurch war memorials, the other being the Citizens' War Memorial in Cathedral Square (currently out of bounds). The Bridge of Remembrance is a title that covers both the bridge over the Ōtākaro Avon River built in 1873 by engineer Edward George Wright (1831–1902) and the memorial arch at the bridge's east end, a competition-winning design by William Henry Gummer, then of the Wellington-based firm Gummer and Prouse. Steeped in Beaux-Arts classicism, gifted and prolific, Gummer is one of the outstanding figures in New Zealand architecture. Before the First World War, he worked in London for Edwin Lutyens (1869–1944), the pre-eminent British architect of his time, and in Chicago for the practice founded by Daniel Burnham (1846–1912), one of the most prominent American architects of the pre-First World War decades.

Gummer's arch is made of concrete faced with Tasmanian stone; reputedly, the faces and planes of the arch express hexagonal angles, or divisions of such angles. The design could keep easy company with structures from Lutyens' extensive post-war votive catalogue such as the Cenotaph in Whitehall (1920) and the Arch of Remembrance in Leicester (1925). The Christchurch arch's connection to the British Empire's war memorial design language is emphasised by the incorporation of imperial symbols — laurel wreaths, fascines, torches with battle names, the British Lion and coat of arms — carved by Frederick Gurnsey and his young assistant Lawrence Berry (1904–1970).

The Terrace

Oxford Terrace between Cashel and Hereford Streets

Jasmax and NH Architecture, 2018

In the decade before the 2011 Christchurch earthquake, Oxford Terrace between Hereford and Cashel streets became known as 'The Strip', a block of bars and restaurants with an atmosphere often described, rather euphemistically, as 'lively'. The row of century-old buildings facing the Ōtākaro Avon River was badly damaged in the 2011 earthquake but, at a time when many hospitality businesses were fleeing the central city, the landowner opted to redevelop and rebrand The Strip. Now, it is 'The Terrace', a suite of mixed-use commercial buildings designed by Jasmax and Australian firm NH Architecture.

The buildings are individual expressions of a site planning model. Rather than being arranged as a line of joined-up buildings, The Terrace is a complex of buildings organised around laneways that, as architects say, 'activate' the interior of the site. 'Porosity' is the principle in play: pedestrian throughways multiply the number of street-level commercial frontages. Melbourne's successful opening-up of its CBD laneways to hospitality use is the precedent being followed at The Terrace.

As for the buildings themselves, they look different, being distinguished by the shape of their forms and the materials of their façades, but they act the same. What they have in common, and what will declare their vintage as surely as Gothic pointed arches or Brutalist concrete beams, are the cantilevered balconies and expanses of glazing offering prospects of the Ōtākaro Avon River.

77 Hereford Street

Warren and Mahoney Architects, 1981

The office building at 77 Hereford Street marks the end of the
mid-career stage of the partnership of the influential architecture
practice led by Miles Warren and Maurice Mahoney. From the
late 1960s Warren and Mahoney had scaled up as the firm began
to receive commissions commensurate with its record and its
ambition. Christchurch Town Hall (1972) and the New Zealand
Chancery building in Washington DC (1979) were the most
prestigious projects of this consolidation phase, but at the same
time that Warren and Mahoney was producing architectural
haute couture the practice was also designing a diffusion range of
Modernist buildings that significantly raised the bar for commercial
architecture in Christchurch.

    The series of seven- to eight-storey pre-cast concrete office
buildings starting with the SIMU Building (1966, demolished
after the 2011 earthquake) and culminating in 77 Hereford Street
(originally the General Accident Building, 1981) typify Warren
and Mahoney's middle years, just as the lineage of small in-situ
concrete and concrete block houses and flats characterised the
practice's youth. What made these otherwise stolid buildings
appealing — and what continues to distinguish 77 Hereford Street
in an increasingly thin-skinned city — was the chiaroscuro effect
of a rhythmic repetition of deeply recessed windows. There was
a functional reason for this façade form: it offered protective
shading to a building without air-conditioning, while also
providing occupants with natural light and views.

Public Trust Office Building

152–156 Oxford Terrace

Cecil Wood, 1925
Historic Place Category 2

Shortly after the February 2011 Christchurch earthquake the government established the Canterbury Earthquake Recovery Authority (CERA) to take charge of the city's (re)development. CERA was given extraordinary discretion, including the power to carry out or order demolition work, at its own behest or that of building owners. It proceeded with considerable alacrity. By February 2014, reported Christchurch's daily newspaper *The Press*, CERA had issued 998 demolition notices. Only five demolition applications had been declined, one of them, for the Public Trust Office, a building occupying a prime site next to the Ōtākaro Avon River near Cathedral Square. Eventually, the building owner succeeded in winning demolition permission but, amidst increasing public agitation for the building's preservation, instead sold it to a developer specialising in heritage conversions. (The same company restored the MED Building, see pages 154–55).

ROUTE 2–34

Thus Christchurch has retained one of the more significant buildings by one of its most prominent architects, Cecil Wood (see index page 221 for his other projects). In the years after the First World War, Wood was a fluent exponent of traditional styles surviving on borrowed time: his houses were neo-Georgian, his churches neo-Gothic and Arts and Crafts, and his commercial buildings neo-Classical. The latter august style certainly seemed appropriate for the Christchurch branch of a government agency that had been set up in 1872 to safeguard deceased estates from unscrupulous administration. Wood's symmetrical design for the Public Trust Office features on its façade six tall Tuscan pilasters resting on a base of Sydney sandstone and centred on an entrance surmounted by an impressively scaled version of the British Crown's lion-and-unicorn coat of arms, carved by Frederick Gurnsey. The renovation (2020) by Three Sixty Architecture added a rooftop bar above the building's parapet and dentilled cornice.

Municipal Chambers — Our City Ōtautahi

159 Oxford Terrace and Worcester Boulevard

Samuel Hurst Seager, 1887
Historic Place Category 1

If Christchurch architecture is a relay — and a respect for lineage is a characteristic of the city — then Samuel Hurst Seager would be first baton change. Benjamin Mountfort employed Seager; Seager hired Cecil Wood; Wood employed Miles Warren. This is a very strong line-up, and Seager certainly justifies his place. He started on 'the tools' in his father's Christchurch building company. When his father died in 1874, he took over the firm — he was 19 at the time — and built the first Canterbury College buildings for Mountfort. Seager then worked for the architect and attended Canterbury College before continuing his studies in London. On his return to Christchurch he announced his presence by winning the 1885 competition to design the city's Municipal Chambers.

Seager's competition entry, portentously titled 'Design with Beauty: Build with Truth' — the phrase is the motto of his London alma mater, the Architectural Association — was in the decorative and eclectic Queen Anne style that was enjoying a comeback in Britain. The design featured four differentiated façades and incorporated the figures of 'Industry' and 'Concord', early works by English sculptor George Frampton (1860–1928). It was all too much for some Christchurch critics, and Mountfort had to vouch for the building. Seager went on to design gentry homes, model workers' houses and New Zealand war memorials, including those at Le Quesnoy, Messines and Chunuk Bair. He taught architecture and design at Canterbury College, and his promotion of town planning significantly contributed to the 1926 Town Planning Act. Seager was also an authority on art gallery lighting, an advocate for heritage preservation, and a champion of professional standards in architecture. The repair of the earthquake-damaged Municipal Chambers is a fitting tribute to his legacy.

Canterbury Provincial Government Buildings

280 Durham Street North, Armagh Street and Gloucester Street

Benjamin Mountfort, 1858–1865
Historic Place Category 1

In architecture, as in everything else, achievement depends on both talent and timing. In colonial Christchurch, Benjamin Mountfort had the opportunity to make the most of his ability, and he took it, designing numerous significant buildings in the course of a long career that established his reputation as the city's architectural founding father. Mountfort arrived in Christchurch from England in 1850 as a young Gothic Revival architect, and his great good fortune was that the style in which he was so proficient endured locally until his death. In the late 1850s, Mountfort and his brother-in-law Isaac Luck (1817–1881) were the official architects for the Canterbury settlement when they received the plum commission to design a building to house the Provincial Council.

The job turned into a three-stage project, expanding with Canterbury's rapidly increasing wealth. The initial timber building, centred on a council chamber modelled on late medieval English manorial halls, soon received an extension featuring a stone tower, and a stone council chamber was added in 1865. By this time, Mountfort was briefly in partnership with Maxwell Bury (1825–1912), a Nottinghamshire-born engineer who later designed the University of Otago's iconic Gothic Revival Clocktower Building (1879). The dramatic council chamber, with its encaustic tiles, sandstone walls and stained glass windows from the London firm of Lavers & Barraud, was to become Mountfort's most acclaimed work, along with Canterbury College's Great Hall (pages 24–25). Along with the central stone tower, the council chamber was destroyed in the 2011 earthquake; much of the timber structure survives.

ROUTE 3: SOUTH

The south side of the CBD, historically home to foundries and small businesses, is becoming a vibrant residential and commercial district. Hine-Pāka, the main city bus station, and Te Omeka, the juridical and emergency services complex, were early 'anchor' projects in the Christchurch recovery. Further east, numerous projects in and around Lichfield and High streets, several of them in restored heritage buildings, are succeeding in putting back together what was a diverting and humanly scaled district. The emerging Christchurch trend of finer-grain urban development featuring laneways and small courtyards is clearly evident in the area.

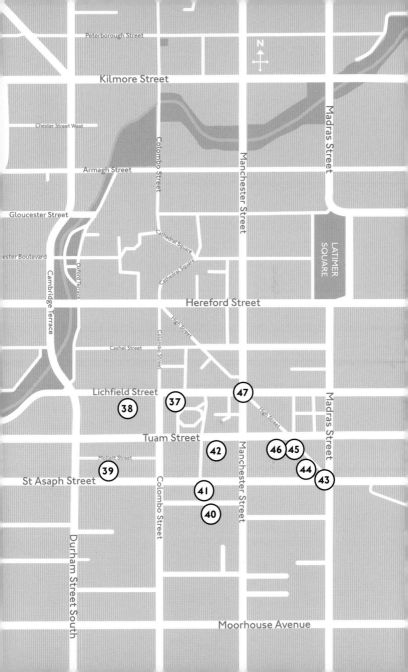

Te Omeka Justice and Emergency Services Precinct

20 Lichfield Street

Warren and Mahoney Architects,
Cox Architecture, Opus Architecture, 2017

The Christchurch Justice and Emergency Services Precinct was an 'anchor' project in the city's post-2011 reconstruction. Designed by Warren and Mahoney Architects, with Australian prison and police station specialist Cox Architecture and New Zealand infrastructure consultants Opus Architecture, the three-building precinct combines juridical institutions and emergency services — courts, police, corrections, fire and ambulance services — in a 42,000-square-metre complex occupying a city block and surrounding a central courtyard. The administrative centralisation facilitated by the precinct is a post-earthquake strategy to strengthen civic resilience, but the project was also an opportunity to design spaces that suit and signal contemporary function.

This modernising impulse is most evident in the treatment of the law courts. In contrast to the former Christchurch Law Courts (see pages 162–63), with its convoluted organisation of cramped courtrooms and offices, the new courts building is arranged more generously and transparently around an atrium with views out to the city and the Port Hills. The precinct is a behemoth with a butch façade — a jutting display of concrete and glass boxes — but a more sensitive interior. 'It's light and airy,' acknowledged one local judge, before putting on his black cap to add, 'but I wanted dark and scary.' More profoundly, a higher-ranked judge expressed his opposition to the Justice Precinct's disregard for the principle that the courts and the police are arms of government that are, and must be seen to be, separate.

Hine-Pāka Christchurch Bus Interchange

Corner Lichfield Street and Colombo Street

Architectus, 2015

While railway stations in New Zealand's big cities were monuments that declared a pride in their purpose, bus stations have commonly expressed nothing but civic parsimony. In large part, the difference was down to the calendar of the country's development. A century ago, the railway connected the nation; train travel was significant, and a city's train station was both primary portal and status symbol. Buses, when they came along, decades later, were just another transport mode, serving carless urban commuters and less affluent inter-city travellers. Bus stations, where they existed, were desultory waiting or loitering areas from which cold draughts never managed to dispel foul air.

This history explains why the Hine-Pāka Christchurch Bus Interchange is such a welcome surprise. The building — and thank goodness its lifeless English title has been animated by the name of a Ngāi Tahu ancestor — was the first Christchurch post-earthquake 'anchor' project and it set a reassuring precedent for new public architecture in the city.

Designed by Architectus, a practice of Auckland origins with a strong portfolio of Christchurch buildings (see also pages 108–09, 134–35 and 142–49), the bus station is an L-shaped building that wraps around a prominent city corner to provide comfortable shelter — underfloor heating! natural light! clean toilets! — and easy access to bus platforms. The dramatic folded roof provides generous internal volume and signals the building's presence, and is also a hat-tip to the local Gothic tradition.

Ao Tawhiti Building

5 Mollett Street

Stephenson & Turner, 2019

All schools have 'character', but some schools proclaim their particularity more overtly than others. In Christchurch, the city's oldest school, Christ's College, is the archetype of the traditional 'character' school, its identity expressed through archaic uniforms, arcane rituals and 170 years of careful stewardship of its architectural stock. This is character by accretion, but character can also be a matter of contrivance. Christchurch's newest school, Ao Tawhiti — in longform, Ao Tawhiti Unlimited Discovery — is a 'designated character school'. This type of school belongs to the state education system but has considerable discretion in pursuing its own course, which in Ao Tawhiti's case is 'self-directed learning'.

Ao Tawhiti, which combines primary and secondary school students in one big building, is resolutely a central-city school and was a pioneering presence in the now more rapidly developing 'South Frame' of the city's post-earthquake urban blueprint. Ao Tawhiti doesn't have any grounds; instead, it treats the city as its campus by piggybacking on civic amenities such as parks and libraries. The building exemplifies the contemporary blurring of educational and commercial architecture. A steel and concrete structure, with a façade of terracotta tiles and irregular fenestration, surrounds a central atrium that connects four floors of flexible spaces. The building was designed by Stephenson & Turner, an architectural and engineering practice of Australian origin that came to New Zealand in 1956 and specialised in designing larger-scale Modernist buildings. The company no longer exists in Australia, but in New Zealand it continues to add to an extensive portfolio of commercial and institutional projects.

Atlas Quarter

36 Welles Street

Architectus and DKO, 2019

The blocks south of the East Frame, around the intersection of Manchester and St Asaph streets (the latter named for a possibly apocryphal sixth-century Welsh bishop), have emerged as the liveliest precinct in the Christchurch urban revival, which is still very much a work in progress. The area increasingly is the site of housing intensification projects intended to return residents to the central city. Among these schemes is Atlas Quarter, three apartment buildings and a townhouse mews deployed along the north–south axis of a deep rectangular site. The combination of building typologies is reminiscent of a scheme in Auckland's waterfront Wynyard Quarter designed by Architectus, the practice that, together with DKO, is responsible for Atlas Quarter. (Not that precedents from Auckland are loudly proclaimed in Christchurch.)

Where the Wynyard Quarter project comprises an 11-level apartment tower, five-level pavilion and three-level mews, Atlas Quarter has a three-level apartment building — which also serves as the site portal — and a mews of two-level townhouses (both DKO), and two five-level apartment buildings (Architectus). The separation between the mews and the two larger apartment buildings is well handled to admit daylight into the heart of Atlas Quarter and allow relaxed pedestrian passage.

Atlas Quarter is named for the Atlas Foundry, which occupied the site from 1876 until the later decades of the twentieth century. The foundry was built by the pioneering Christchurch engineering company founded by the Scott brothers, John Lee (1848–1913) and George (1852–1930), migrants from Derby, where their family ran an ironworks, the original Atlas Foundry, and where, in Derby Town Hall in the late 1860s, they fatefully heard former Governor Sir George Grey praising the wonders of New Zealand. Christchurch's Atlas Foundry made steam locomotives, bridges and viaducts, and, in the Second World War, several million grenades, but became best known for its Atlas domestic ovens and stoves.

P & D Duncan Building

204 St Asaph Street

Clarkson and Ballantyne, 1903
Historic Place Category 2

In 1877 the Christchurch railway station — no longer extant — was built on a site halfway along Moorhouse Avenue. Over several subsequent decades, the area north of the station developed as an industrial area, occupied by factories of the hard-core Victorian and Edwardian variety — forges, foundries and ironmongers. The P & D Duncan Building is a rare survivor from this heavy metal era. The building was constructed for a company specialising in the manufacture of agricultural machinery, established in the 1870s by brothers Peter (1838–1907) and David (1832–1897) Duncan, Scottish migrants who were skilled smiths and devout Presbyterians. By the turn of the century, the firm was led by the next Duncan generation, who commissioned a new foundry on St Asaph Street.

The building was designed by the practice led by William Albert Paxton Clarkson (1863–1917), son of an early Canterbury colonist, and Australian-born Robert Anderson Ballantyne (1866–1936). When the three-storeyed P & D Duncan Building opened in 1904 — the date inscribed on the parapet suggests a lag between completion and occupancy — it was described by the local *Lyttelton Times* as 'handsome and imposing as well as very substantial'. And so it remains, with its symmetrical fenestration, warm brick façade ornamented with banding and keystones in Ōamaru stone, and arcuated parapets emphasising its terminus at both ends. The building is complemented in style by its smaller immediate neighbour, also a foundry (by architect William Wilson), built in 1904 for R. Buchanan & Sons, another company of Scottish origin and an amicable competitor to the Duncans. In 1986, P & D Duncan Ltd, by then no longer in family ownership, closed. A decade later, the P & D Duncan Building was converted into apartments and ground-floor retail tenancies by Warren and Mahoney, and after suffering earthquake damage it was restored to such use by Jerram Tocker Barron Architects (2019).

Environment Canterbury Building

200 Tuam Street

Wilson & Hill Architects, 2016

Environment Canterbury, often shortened to the even hipper term ECan, is the brand name of Canterbury Regional Council, which has responsibility for many aspects of land and water use in the largest of New Zealand's administrative regions. Regional councils may have far less discretion than their Provincial Government forebears enjoyed in their nineteenth-century heyday, but they still have significant clout. Environment Canterbury, for example, has jurisdiction of all the river catchments in a 4-million-hectare area that stretches for 400 kilometres from the Clarence River in the north to the Waitaki River in the south. That puts the elected body at the centre of the water politics of a farming area that has undergone rapid, and very thirsty, intensification in the last 20 years.

For Environment Canterbury, the second decade of the twenty-first century was a tough time. In 2010, the National government used policy differences among elected councillors as the *casus belli* to dismiss councillors and replace them with unelected commissioners — a fully elected council was not returned to office until 2019 — and in the 2010–2011 earthquakes Environment Canterbury's premises were badly damaged.

The organisation's new building, designed by Wilson & Hill Architects, is an exemplar of post-quake architecture. The five-storey building, which accommodates 450 staff, rests on piles driven 16 metres into the ground and employs base isolation and superstructural flexibility to provide earthquake resistance. Resistance to political interference? That's another story.

Boxed Quarter

St Asaph Street and Madras Street

Field Studio of Architecture + Urbanism, 2017

The rebuilding of earthquake-damaged Christchurch quickly became a top-down exercise led by central government, principally via the Canterbury Earthquake Recovery Authority (CERA), which was established just a month after the February 2011 earthquake. In the arena of the central city, CERA for five years had the life-and-death power of Commodus in the Colosseum: buildings were condemned or saved on CERA's say-so. (As a rule, the imperial thumb was turned down.) The bossy bureaucratisation of the Christchurch rebuild was understandable — big disaster, small country — but was not only an explicit judgment on the capacity and competence of the council; it also betrayed an impatience with the processes of local democracy. However, although the council may have been sidelined, the community did not passively surrender all of its agency. The most optimistic phenomenon of the early rebuild years was an occupy movement, tolerated at first and later sanctioned, that activated empty lots with temporary installations, dozens of them — gardens, book exchanges, pop-up stores, a mobile dance-floor, a pallet pavilion.

Many of these initiatives were instigated by the young activists of the Gap Filler Trust. Not all of the projects by members of Gap Filler, which is now a recognised part of the Christchurch urban design system, were micro-sized. The most ambitious was Boxed Quarter, a three- and four-storey cluster of steel-framed rectangular modules on the corner of St Asaph and Madras streets. The small-business precinct is the large-scale realisation of a prefabricated construction system designed by Gap Filler co-founder Andrew Just when he worked for local company F3 Design and then developed under the auspices of his own practice, Field Studio of Architecture + Urbanism. Boxed Quarter has some formal and material affinities to RE:START, a temporary mall constructed from shipping containers that from 2011 to 2018 was a morale-boosting presence on Cashel Street in the retail heart of the city.

135 High Street and Duncan's Buildings

AE Architects, 2021; Luttrell Brothers, 1905
Historic Place Category 2 (Duncan's Buildings)

Filling a post-earthquake gap next to an Edwardian two-storey brick terrace, steel-faced 135 High Street observes the existing building's height-line but accommodates an extra floor. Such intervention often disrupts a streetscape, but by continuing the lines of the terrace's cornices, architrave and parapet across the façade of the new building, AE Architects have established a harmonious relationship between the neighbours. The double-sided nature of the site, which borders both High and St Asaph streets, provides the new building with two public faces, both clad with a rain-screen of weathered steel, a material much-loved by architects for its texture and atavistic industrial connotations.

135 High Street has inherited the DNA of a neighbourhood which, throughout the twentieth century, was populated by small shops and businesses. Duncan's Buildings, the terrace that is punctuated by 135 High Street and which now exists only as a façade, was designed for this petit-bourgeois ecosystem by the Luttrell brothers (see pages 128–29). The row of 16 (now 13) street-level shops with upper-level flats may have been a bread-and-butter commission, but the Luttrells doled out some drama in the form of paired bays of arched windows, an entablature and central pediment. The terrace was commissioned by a Whanganui family trust associated with Elizabeth Robertson Duncan (?–1917), and sold in the wake of a great scandal: in 1920, Charles Mackay (1875–1929), the progressive mayor of Whanganui, and husband of Robertson's daughter, Isobel, was jailed for shooting — not fatally — D'Arcy Cresswell (1896–1960), a one-time employee of Christchurch architecture practice Collins and Harman and later a poet and journalist, who was subjecting him to homosexual blackmail. Exiled from New Zealand, Mackay was working in Berlin as a reporter for the London *Daily Express* in May 1929 when he was killed by police who had opened fire on a Red Front demonstration.

A. J. White's Building

181 High Street and Tuam Street

England Brothers, 1910
Historic Place Category 2 (façade)

Façadism, the practice of retaining some or even all of a building's exterior while otherwise replacing the whole structure, deservedly gets a bad rap. Inevitably, it seems to involve the betrayal of the integrity of an old building and the distortion of its successor. Everyone — heritage advocates, council officers, architects — knows this, but agrees to façade preservation as a compromise serving a greater good. Façadism might not do a building many favours, but that's not the point: it's a conciliarity gesture to the street. And now and then it's worth it. The restored Edwardian façade that wraps around the corner of High and Tuam streets signifies a prominent site and pays homage to the historic character of a part of Christchurch particularly distressed in the 2010–2011 earthquakes.

The three-storey façade is an exuberant design by the practice established by the England brothers, Robert William (1863–1908) and Edward Herbert (1875–1949). For the undoctrinaire Englands, each building commission offered a variety of design options; it was like being presented with a mixed tray of equally delectable chocolates. At 181 High Street, the firm selected Ōamaru stone piers, contrasting upper-floor window treatments on either side of a rusticated band of projecting stonework, leaded fanlights and an oriel above the main entrance at the building's apex corner. And lots of glazing, to display the household wares sold by A. J. White's, a firm founded by English migrants Alfred (1837–1895) and Eliza (1841–1909) White, he a Catholic and she a Protestant — a distinction that mattered in colonial New Zealand — and both of them commercially astute philanthropists (Eliza ecumenically funded a Catholic orphanage). In 1980 the landmark building passed into the ownership of retailer McKenzie & Willis; severely earthquake damaged, it was redeveloped and extensively altered. Conservation architect Dave Pearson supervised the restoration of its façade (2019).

Post and Telegraph Office

185 High Street

John Thomas Mair, 1932

If you prefer Art Deco in its vertical forms, rather than the horizontal residential iterations that pepper-pot New Zealand suburbia, the former Post and Telegraph Office on the corner of High and Tuam streets is a building for you. It looks good these days, having been restored, strengthened and adapted to house a cinema and café by owners who bought it from the government when the state sold off assets in the 1980s. The building was designed by John Thomas (J. T.) Mair (1876–1959), who served as Government Architect from 1923 to 1941, a period in which concrete and steel were replacing brick and timber in larger-scale New Zealand architecture and Modernism was receiving a cautious welcome.

Dexterous in his craft and diligent in character, Mair designed post offices and courthouses up and down the country, and such fine landmark buildings as the Spanish Mission-style Blue Baths in Rotorua (1929), and the Moderne-style Stout Street Departmental Building in Wellington (1937) and Jean Batten Place Departmental Building in Auckland (1942).

Mair, who was born in Invercargill, studied architecture at the University of Pennsylvania (1906–1908). Before returning to New Zealand, he topped up his education with a tour of Classical and Romanesque European architecture, an experience that may have informed his unironic deployment of pilasters and festoons on the façade of the Post and Telegraph Office. Perhaps he was allowing himself a little indulgence; his Cambridge Terrace Post Office (1930) in Wellington, larger and a little earlier, is a far more austere version of Art Deco, its presence derivative from its massing, not its motifs.

Stranges and Glendenning Hill Building

Corner High Street and Lichfield Street

Sheppard & Rout Architects, 2014

At the turn of the twentieth century, the corner where High Street meets Lichfield Street as it cuts diagonally across the city grid was the busiest intersection in Christchurch. The site was occupied by the thriving department store — then New Zealand's largest — of Strange and Company. William Strange (1832–1914) was an immigrant draper whose retail business eventually employed 600 people; he also owned a factory and, for a decade, a 10,000-acre farm on the Selwyn River. On the sides of the V where High Street and Lichfield Street meet, Strange had commissioned from the leading Christchurch architecture practice founded by William Barnett Armson a series of Italianate buildings, culminating in the four-storey block clad in Ōamaru stone that sat at the apex of the triangular site. After Strange's death, his company slowly foundered, and this latter building became one of many Christchurch heritage buildings, especially in this part of the city, whose architectural merit was unrewarded by profitable use.

When the Strange's building was ruined by the 2010 and 2011 earthquakes it was replaced, in a spectacular deposition of stone by steel and glass, with a building designed by Sheppard & Rout Architects, and seismically engineered to 180 per cent of the building code. In a small-scale way, the building internalises the old bustle of the High Street / Lichfield Street corner through the incorporation of laneways — a popular contemporary urban design trope — that lead to a sheltered courtyard served by cafés and bars. Sheppard & Rout was founded in 1982 by David Sheppard (b.1942) and Jonty Rout (1947–2003), and has developed into one of the leading Christchurch architecture practices. Sheppard was one of the authors of the 2012 'Blueprint' for the city's recovery.

ROUTE 4: EAST

The most visible reminder of the destruction of the 2010–2011 earthquakes is the ruined ChristChurch Cathedral, the focal point of Christchurch's historic city centre. While the debate over the cathedral's fate raged — it has now been settled in favour of restoration — other damaged buildings were restored, and the 'Cardboard' Cathedral was quickly constructed a few blocks away. This route includes two significant 'anchor' projects — Tūranga (the Christchurch Central Library) and Te Pae (the convention centre). There's also a street of Spanish Mission shops, a restored Edwardian theatre, a large and popular playground, and the East Frame precinct of medium-density housing.

New Regent Street

Henry Francis Willis, 1932
Historic Place Category 1

In an architecturally serious city in which the bar was set early, and high, by Benjamin Mountfort's High Victorian Gothic Revivalism, New Regent Street is a surprising incidence of design levity. Along its 100-metre length, the pedestrianised street, which connects Gloucester and Armagh streets, is lined with two-storeyed, pastel-coloured terraced shops, alternately topped by a curly gable or a straight-edged canopy. It looks make-believe — a film set, perhaps, or a piece of townscape conceived by Disney imagineers.

This fantastical quality is not accidental. The designer of New Regent Street — named, presumably, after the famous London shopping street — was Henry Francis Willis (1892/93–1972), a Christchurch architect who specialised in cinemas. Willis brought his theatrical sensibility to the design of New Regent Street, and also a determination to give the project, which was developed as a kind of outdoor mall with 40 shops, a unifying coherence. These impulses combined in Willis's stylistic treatment of the project. He opted for Spanish Mission, which, after having been deployed sparingly for 20 years in New Zealand, enjoyed a sudden vogue, especially in Napier and Hasting as those cities were rebuilt after the 1931 earthquake. There's something sunny about the Spanish Mission style (it came from California, after all); in the midst of the Depression, it promised the welcome escapism of a movie from the Hollywood dream factory.

After the 2011 earthquake, Fulton Ross Team Architects directed the street's restoration (2013). Also restored was the tram line in the middle of the street; the rails serve the heritage tram that since the mid-1990s has followed a route through the western part of the central city.

Isaac Theatre Royal

145 Gloucester Street

Alfred and Sidney Luttrell, 1908
Historic Place Category 1

The Theatre Royal is the third incarnation of a theatre of this name on Gloucester Street and the second on this site. It was commissioned from the Australian-born and -trained Luttrell brothers, Alfred (1865–1924), who was the designer in the family, and Sidney (1872–1932), who supervised construction and dealt with clients. In this case, the client was a syndicate, headed by American actor and impresario James Cassius Williamson (1845–1913), that owned a chain of theatres in Australia and New Zealand. The Theatre Royal was retro, even in 1908: the Luttrell brothers took a form-advertises-function approach and styled the building in a theatrical Victorian manner. In the late 1920s the building was turned into a cinema, but in the 1950s it once more became a performance venue, serving up, for several decades, a democratic bill of fare — operas, ballets, concerts, wrestling matches, magic shows.

A public campaign saved the building from demolition in the late 1970s and it was restored as a working theatre in 2004–2005 and again, far more substantially, after the 2010 and 2011 earthquakes (Warren and Mahoney Architects, lead architect Richard McGowan, with Vanessa Carswell, 2014). The most obvious of the extensions associated with post-quakes restoration is the expressly contemporary addition on the building's west side.

A feature of the Rococo interior of the theatre, which now bears the name of civic benefactor Diana Isaac (1921–2012), is the dome with its original decoration — scenes from *A Midsummer Night's Dream*, painted by G. C. Post of Wellington's Carrara Ceiling Company, channelling his inner Tiepolo. The mural was restored under the direction of conservator Carolina Izzo.

Te Pae

188 Oxford Terrace

Woods Bagot, with Warren and Mahoney Architects and Matapopore Trust, 2021

In New Zealand cities, Auckland excepted, infrastructure projects tend to occur serially, the cities being small and the projects complex. Post-earthquake Christchurch definitely bucked this trend. The Central City Recovery Plan — the 'Blueprint' — adopted in 2012 called for the rapid and often simultaneous development of 'anchor' projects. Some proceeded relatively smoothly — the Justice and Emergency Services Precinct (pages 102–03), for example, and the Bus Interchange (pages 104–05). But two proved controversial: the convention centre and the sports stadium. New convention centres and stadiums are contentious everywhere; they're always accompanied by arguments about economic priorities and cultural hegemony. It doesn't help that the case for such facilities usually comes down to a fingers-crossed evocation of best-case scenarios. And then there's the climate crisis, and a global pandemic — perhaps not extinction events for conference centres and stadiums, but credible threats to their sustainability.

Anyway: the Christchurch Convention Centre, or Te Pae, the polysemous Māori word here interpreted as 'a gathering space', was designed by Australian practice Woods Bagot, working with Warren and Mahoney and the Matopopore Trust. The 28,000-square-metre, two-level building occupies two former city blocks to the north of Cathedral Square. (This siting required the city grid surrender a section of Gloucester Street.) Design architect Bruno Mendes was inspired by an aerial view of Canterbury's foothills and braided rivers — the latters' forms are certainly suggested by Te Pae's sinuous slither across its site, and their coloration by the 43,000 speckled tiles on the building's façade. (A nod, perhaps, to the celebrated chevron tile-work on the most famous building in this part of the world — Jørn Utzon's Sydney Opera House.) Te Pae relates far better to the city on its north side than its south, where, for now, there's nothing much to connect with.

Tūranga

60 Cathedral Square

**Architectus, Schmidt Hammer Lassen Architects
and Matapopore Trust, 2018**

In the first years of post-earthquake reconstruction there was
considerable global interest in the questions of what form the new
Christchurch central city might take and what sort of architecture
might emerge on the *tabula rasa* of bulldozed city blocks. It seemed
that this interest, and a steady parade of overseas experts, would
yield a crop of buildings designed by international practices, and
that a relatively parochial city could take on, for better or worse, a
cosmopolitan architectural character.

But this did not happen; apart from Shigeru Ban, whose
presence was the result of peculiar circumstances (see pages
150–51), the only exotic architectural practice to have been
involved in a major Christchurch recovery project is Schmidt
Hammer Lassen Architects, a Danish firm that is a world-leader
in library architecture. In partnership with Architectus and the
Matapopore Trust, which represents local iwi Ngāi Tahu and hapū
Ngāi Tūāhuriri, it designed Tūranga, the central Christchurch library.

The anchor building is a five-storey civic marker on an important
site that, pre-earthquake, was shared, in desultory fashion, by
God (via ChristChurch Cathedral) and Mammon (in the guise of
various tourist traps). Tūranga is a milestone in the evolution of
biculturalism in a city in which Anglocentrism has at times blurred
into racial chauvinism. The library acknowledges local iwi not
only in its title — Tūranga is the name of a Ngāi Tahu ancestral
settlement — but also through the realisation, most obvious in the
library's dramatic and generous central stairway, of the concept of
whakamanuhiri, the welcoming or 'bringing-in' of visitors.

ChristChurch Cathedral

Cathedral Square

George Gilbert Scott, Benjamin Mountfort, 1864–1904
Historic Place Category 1

ChristChurch Cathedral has long enjoyed the status of civic symbol, but latterly it attracted a different sort of attention as the focus of the post-earthquake debate about heritage preservation. Actually, 'debate' is too tame a term for the vitriolic exchange of opinions, between savers and scrappers, about the fate of the badly damaged Church of England cathedral. (A complete account of this episode would require a Trollopian grasp of feline ecclesiastical politics.) The building reduced to rubble in the 2011 earthquake was designed by the English Gothic Revival architect George Gilbert Scott, senior, with considerable later input by Benjamin Mountfort.

Scott's original design for the cathedral — the epicentre of Anglicanism in New Zealand's most Anglican city — was for a cost-conscious and earthquake-resistant timber church, but the Bishop of Christchurch, Henry Harper (1804–1893), wanted a stone building. On-site supervision of construction, which began in 1864, was carried out by Robert Speechly and, following his departure from Christchurch in 1868, by Benjamin Mountfort. Over the years, Mountfort made changes to Scott's design — on the exterior, where he substituted stone for timber in the spire, and especially in the interior, where he designed much of the furniture and a number of stained glass windows. When Mountfort died in 1898, his son Cyril saw the project through to its 1904 conclusion.

In 2017, after a litigious post-earthquake interlude, the local Anglican synod resolved to restore, not replace, the cathedral; completion is expected in 2027. The statue of John Robert Godley (1814–1861), 'The Founder of Canterbury', presumably will retain its privileged position in Cathedral Square.

Old Government Building

28 Cathedral Square and Worcester Street

Joseph Clarkson Maddison, 1913
Historic Place Category 1

The Government Building — sometimes referred to in the plural
— was commissioned by the pro-public works Liberal government
led by Sir Joseph Ward (1856–1930) to house the Christchurch
offices of central government departments. For some reason, the
design job did not go to the Government Architect, Edwardian
Baroque aficionado John Campbell (1857–1942). Instead, it went
to local architect Joseph Clarkson Maddison (1850–1923), an
English migrant who had arrived in Christchurch in 1872, who may
have been chosen because he possessed big-building experience —
hotels and freezing works were his specialties — or perhaps some
design devolution was deemed politic.

Maddison was an Italianate dissenter from Christchurch's
Gothic Revival orthodoxy. 'He mastered one style,' writes historian
John Wilson, perhaps a little unkindly, 'and was content to work
within its rather narrow limits.' However Maddison won the
Government Building project, he certainly seems to have relished
his opportunity. He knew how to dress up a big box, and gave the
Government Building the full Italian Renaissance Palazzo treatment:
rusticated stone base; two levels of brick façade punctuated
symmetrically by tall windows in highly articulated frames;
Corinthian entablature and a parapet (now replaced in replica).

There's a lot going on, but the standout — literally — features
of the building are the columns surmounting the north entrance
and, especially, the extraordinary four-columned recessed
portico (or *portico in antis*) above the west entrance. The building
accommodated government departments for 70 years until it
was abandoned during the state asset-shedding of the late 1980s.
It was threatened with demolition until the city council bought it
and then sold it to developers. In its restored state, the building
functions as a hotel.

2 Cathedral Square

Sheppard & Rout Architects, 2020

Cathedral Square was a conundrum well before the collapse of its focal structure in 2011 further complicated its disposition and functionality. In the decades before the earthquakes, the square struggled to live up to its billing as the heart of Christchurch. Over that time, its activation was effectively outsourced to English migrant Ian Brackenbury Channell who, in character as the 'Wizard of Christchurch', staged eccentric theatrics before lunchtime audiences. Cosmetic changes to the square, including new paving, were controversial but not transformative, an outcome that suggests deeper-seated problems connected to planning and contextual relationships.

These issues go way back. The original 1850 Christchurch plan envisaged the square as a cruciform — an appropriate shape for an Anglican settlement — encompassing both a cathedral and Christ's College. But the college was built elsewhere (see pages 38–59), and roads driven through the plan whittled the square's cross-shape into more of a parallelogram. This outcome perhaps supports the argument that the public space New Zealand is most comfortable with is not the square but the cross-roads. A lesson of history, though, from the piazzas of medieval and Renaissance Italy to the quad at Christ's College, is that squares work best if their defining buildings are collectively commissioned by institutions — communes or signorie, churches or colleges — with discretionary power and a long-term perspective.

Cathedral Square has not had these advantages. The cathedral will be rebuilt and the council has realised the excellent Tūranga (see pages 134–35), but the success of the square also depends on the quality and contextual contribution of privately commissioned buildings. The latest project of such provenance is sited at the square's south-east corner. Designed by Sheppard & Rout Architects, the five-storey building, extensively glazed above the pilotis-enabled undercroft, is organised around two atriums, one featuring a dramatic staircase winding its way through the corporate void.

East Frame Housing

Huanui Lane between Gloucester and Lichfield Streets

Architectus; AW Architects; Context; Sheppard & Rout Architects; Warren and Mahoney Architects, 2017–2021

In December 2011, Christchurch City Council presented a plan for the rebuilding of the central city to the responsible minister in the National Party-led government, Gerry Brownlee. Brownlee rejected the plan, established the Canterbury Earthquake Recovery Authority (CERA, see page 95), and gave it 100 days to devise a new plan. This plan, dubbed the 'Blueprint', was produced by a consortium comprising architecture practices of local origin (Warren and Mahoney Architects and Sheppard & Rout Architects) and foreign provenance (Woods Bagot and Populous), landscaping company Boffa Miskell and project manager RCP. The market-oriented government approved the unapologetically interventionist Blueprint, which compressed the area of the rebuilt city by inserting 'frames' that defined the north, south and east sides of the city centre. (Hagley Park serves, de facto, as the west frame.)

Framing promoted the economic and social viability of the CBD by restricting the amount of land available for immediate development on its edges. Although not overtly, perhaps even coincidentally, the compression that is the guiding principle of the Blueprint addressed a fundamental historic condition of central Christchurch: its lack of containment. That's what can happen when planners — surveyors, more properly — impose an urban grid on a flat plain. In 1975, Miles Warren, Christchurch's pre-eminent architect of the second half of the twentieth century, considered the legacy of the 1850 town plan produced for the Canterbury Association by surveyors Joseph Thomas (1803–?) and Edward Jollie (1825–1894). The siting of the Christchurch settlement, and the drawing up of parallel streets of uniformly generous width, Warren wrote, bequeathed 'a town that bleeds away to nothing'. While Hagley Park established a boundary on the city's west side, in other directions, especially to the east, 'the city just runs down, physically and architecturally'. Instances of 'man-made

containment' were rare, Warren noted, the outstanding exceptions to the norm of urban diffusion being the buildings grouped together at Christ's College, Canterbury College (now the Arts Centre) and the Municipal Chambers.

The Blueprint's strategy of containment is most clearly discernible in the east frame, half a dozen blocks bordered by Madras Street to the east, Manchester Street to the west, Lichfield Street to the south and the Ōtākaro Avon River to the north. In the Blueprint, this area was designated as a medium-density housing precinct. Slowly at first, but latterly more steadily, the large rectangle of demolition-cleared land has come under development. At the heart of the east frame is Rauora Park, a linear park that stretches for more than 600 metres north–south through the site and is flanked on its east side by Huanui Lane.

This open space provides good views of the adjacent architecture and the close conjunction, in space and time, of same-type projects by different practices inevitably encourages a 'beauty pageant' reading of the buildings on display. Architects are inclined to proclaim their disdain for such shallow evaluation, although you suspect that having to collectively strut their stuff in public does stimulate their competitive instincts; it is certainly an opportunity to advertise their wares.

From north to south, the running order is: Sheppard & Rout (between Gloucester and Worcester streets, see page 146); Warren and Mahoney (between Worcester and Hereford streets, pages 148-49); Context (between Hereford and Cashel streets); AW Architects (between Cashel and Lichfield streets, page 142), and Architectus (also between Cashel and Lichfield streets, to the south, pages 144–45). There are more medium-density townhouses and apartments one block over from Huanui Lane, on Latimer Square.

'Cardboard' Cathedral

234 Hereford Street

Shigeru Ban, with Warren and Mahoney Architects, 2013

The genesis of the Christchurch Transitional or 'Cardboard' Cathedral was so serendipitous that the theistically inclined might call it miraculous. Shortly after the February 2011 earthquake wrecked ChristChurch Cathedral, local Anglican cleric Craig Dixon came across an article about the Japanese architect Shigeru Ban, famous for his design of emergency structures, and then contacted Ban asking what he would charge to design a temporary cathedral in Christchurch.

And so it came to pass that Christchurch now has the only building in New Zealand designed — for no fee — by a winner of international architecture's top personal award, the Pritzker Prize. Of course, the story of the building's realisation was not quite so straightforward, but the project was characterised throughout by goodwill and collegiality, qualities notably absent from the debate about the fate of the 'real' Anglican cathedral.

The article that caught Reverend Dixon's attention focused on a temporary church, made of paper tubes, that Ban had designed in Kobe after the 1995 Great Hanshin earthquake. Ban proposed a similar, although considerably larger, building for Christchurch, but modified the structural design to accommodate local manufacturing capabilities and the church's escalation of the projected life of the 'temporary' 700-seat cathedral from 10 to 50 years.

This is a deceptively sophisticated building. The structure's 98 six-metre-long cardboard tubes are reinforced by timber beams and steel bracing. Up top, a polycarbonate roof twists into hyperbolic paraboloids; underneath, a 900-millimetre concrete raft protects against ground liquefaction. Forty-nine translucent coloured panels designed by Ban and his colleague Yoshie Narimatsu illuminate the dramatic, triangular main façade.

Christchurch Club

154 Worcester Street

Benjamin Mountfort, 1862
Historic Place Category 1

Scarcely had English settlers arrived in Canterbury than they set about creating institutions that would make them feel at home. For a group of wealthy landowners, a gentlemen's club was high on the social agenda. The Christchurch Club was founded by a dozen runholders in 1856 as a city base for the country gentry, a place where business and politics could be transacted — homogeneously, in both a class and a gender sense. (Urban professional and business members soon felt sufficiently alienated to start their own club — the Canterbury Club, see pages 78–79.)

Benjamin Mountfort was appointed to design the Christchurch Club's building, and produced an Italian Villa arrangement of a central tower flanked by two wings. Mountfort historian Ian Lochhead speculates that the use of this style, popular with bourgeois clients in Britain from around 1840 and later in Australasia and America, may have been a compromise between Mountfort's Gothic Revival inclinations and club members' preference for the more formal Italian Palazzo style associated with gentlemen's clubs in London. (They may also have preferred a masonry building, but timber was more conveniently to hand.)

Another historian, Melanie Lovell-Smith, notes, drily, that the perception of the Italian Villa style as 'comparatively informal and as both elegant yet rural' made it 'a suitable combination for a club basing itself on English upper-class institutions but establishing itself in the middle of what was still a swamp'. Damaged in the 2011 earthquake, the building was restored by Warren and Mahoney Architects.

MED Building

200 Armagh Street

Christchurch Municipal Electricity Department, 1933–1939

In defining the boundary between the East Frame and Margaret Mahy Family Playground, the renovated Art Deco/Moderne building that stretches along a substantial reach of Armagh Street makes a valuable contribution to the public realm. Its civic contribution, though, was once far more significant and much more dynamic. The building was commissioned by Christchurch City Council's Municipal Electricity Department (MED) as a substation and converter station that 'converted' incoming high-voltage direct current (DC) electric power into the alternating current (AC) form supplied for consumer use. The power feeding the Armagh Street plant came from the Lake Coleridge hydro-electric station — New Zealand's first major station, initiated by Christchurch City Council but taken over by the government prior to its inauguration in 1914.

The steel-reinforced concrete MED building, which replaced a brick structure rendered suddenly inappropriate by the 1931 Napier earthquake, was constructed in 1933 and extended six years later. It was part of a site that in the 1930s included a council garage, stables and offices, electrical showroom, 'destructor' — which burned rubbish to generate electricity — and public baths. The complex illustrated a Christchurch paradox: New Zealand's most establishment city was also its strongest bastion of municipal socialism. On the MED building, civic good manners prompted the appending of a modestly Classical façade to a very utilitarian structure. The design seems to have been produced in-house under the direction of Edward Hitchcock (1883–1966), a civil and electrical engineer who was the department's general manager from 1920 to 1949. After the deregulation of the electricity sector in the 1980s, the building eventually passed into the ownership of power company Orion — in choosing their names, modern energy companies seem drawn to mythical heroes and old gods — and more latterly a property company that has reconfigured it into exhibition spaces and commercial tenancies.

Tākaro ā Poi Margaret Mahy Family Playground

Ōtākaro Avon River at Manchester Street

Opus International Consultants, with Boffa Miskell, LandLAB, Tina Dyer, Colin Meurk and BDP, 2015

After the September 2010 Christchurch earthquake, a damaging but less destructive event than the 'quake of February 2011, the city council asked the public for ideas to inform the development of a central city recovery plan. More than 100,000 suggestions were submitted, and the strong desire for a 'greener', more accessible and more engaging city found expression in the plan. A few months later, the plan was redundant and the consultative process that shaped it was replaced by a top-down planning regime imposed by central government via the Canterbury Earthquake Recovery Authority (CERA). The new direction for Christchurch redevelopment was set out in the 'Blueprint', produced to meet a 100-day CERA deadline, that compressed the size of the CBD and divided the city into precincts centred on 'anchor' projects.

One of the anchor projects in the East Frame is the 1.6-hectare playground bordered by Manchester and Madras streets, to the west and east, and Armagh Street and the Ōtākaro Avon River, to the south and north. 'Deliberate but managed risk' was the concept for the 'all ages, all abilities' Margaret Mahy Family Playground, which was designed by Opus International Consultants, with landscape practices Boffa Miskell, LandLAB and BDP, playground consultant Tina Dyer and ecologist Colin Meurk, and named for the noted New Zealand author of children's books.

The facility, spacious, vibrant and a world removed from the bleak municipal playgrounds that still litter New Zealand, has been a huge success. It also did its bit for the property sector: the playground itself cost $3 million; the land it occupies cost $20 million to buy, and the same amount to develop.

Oxford Terrace Baptist Church

288 Oxford Terrace

Andrew Barrie Lab, 2017

In the late 1870s, Christchurch Baptists got themselves sufficiently organised to build a substantial church. The congregation held a design competition in 1881 that was won by E. J. Saunders (or Sanders), an architect of elusive biography who seems to have been a local resident, although he was active in Dunedin a few years earlier. The design did not conform to the Gothic Revivalism that had become the house style of an Anglican city. Instead, the Baptists went Classical, opting for a brick building fronted with a stone or rendered masonry pediment-and-columns portico.

The building was not peculiar in its design dissent: a denominational precedent had been set by the Classical Baptist Metropolitan Tabernacle in London (William Willmer Pocock, 1861), and Auckland's Baptist Tabernacle (Edmund Bell, 1885) was also treated to a portico inspired by the Pantheon in Rome. (There is some irony in the Baptists rejecting the architectural tradition of the Church of England only to embrace that of papist Rome.)

In the 2011 earthquake, the Oxford Terrace Baptist Church suffered a spectacular structural collapse. This event forced church authorities to take stock. It's not cynical to suggest that for many Christchurch congregations, which had struggled over recent decades to reconcile heritage architecture and contemporary ecclesiastical practices, the earthquake was a God-given opportunity for a real estate reset. The Baptists of Oxford Terrace now have a modern church of understated form and flexible function designed by Andrew Barrie. Materials from the Modernist palette — concrete, timber and steel — that has served Christchurch well are deployed to appropriately simple effect. History gets a nod in a little parade of columns salvaged from the ruins of the original church.

ROUTE 5: NORTH

This route includes two important buildings designed by Miles Warren, Christchurch's leading architect of the second half of the twentieth century: the Town Hall (restored after a huge citizen campaign) and the early-career Dorset Street Flats. There's also an apartment building designed by Peter Beaven that serves as a reminder that Warren wasn't the only Christ's College old boy with a way with concrete blocks, and a couple of religious buildings that demonstrate Anglicanism wasn't the only confessional game in town. Two monuments of their time — a Gothic Revival teachers' training college and a Brutalist law courts building — present case studies in the challenges of restoration and re-use.

Christchurch Law Courts

Durham Street North and Armagh Street

Government Architect's Office, MoW, 1978–1989

The Christchurch Law Courts is a project that went on for so long its progress seems explicable only in terms of Newtonian physics, specifically the law defining the inertia of objects once set in motion. Which is another way of saying the building was a job carried out by the New Zealand Ministry of Works (MoW). The MoW did a huge amount of work last century but, partly because its schedule was subject to political whim, it often took its time in doing so.

When the Christchurch Law Courts was finally completed in 1989 (with a single tower, not the planned two), one of its architects, Gordon Cullinan, reportedly said he had been working on the building for 21 years. What this meant is that when the building was finished it already seemed anachronistic. If it had been built when it was designed, the Law Courts would have been part of the Christchurch Brutalist architectural family, a sibling to structures at the University of Canterbury's Ilam campus such as the Matariki (Registry) and Puaka-James Hight Buildings (see pages 192–93).

The MoW's design intentions for the Law Courts were admirable. The building's architects made respectful reference to the adjacent Christchurch Town Hall (see pages 164–65), formally, in the cantilever of the low-rise administration block (1978), and materially in the concrete aggregate which both projects sourced from the same quarry. The Law Courts building wasn't cheap — it was made of quality concrete and has copper roofs — and is very strong; it also has a great riverside site. But the building is empty now, and unloved, and no one seems to know quite what to do with it.

Christchurch Town Hall

86 Kilmore Street

Warren and Mahoney, 1972; restored 2019
Historic Place Category 1

The Christchurch Town Hall is so synonymous with Miles Warren you'd think he was destined to design it. Not quite; the design commission for what was only the second post-Second World War town hall in New Zealand was the result of a 58-entry competition that legend has conflated into a showdown between the two largest personalities in Christchurch post-war architecture, Warren and Peter Beaven. (In fact, Beaven's submission did not make it onto the shortlist of five finalists.) But Warren really wanted the job; he knew what the Christchurch Town Hall could mean for his firm, his career and his reputation. The phone call in June 1966, informing him of his competition win, was time-stopping. 'Taking that call,' Warren wrote, 40 years later, 'remains the most exciting moment of my life.'

The Town Hall is not a singular building, but rather a composition of structures — the main auditorium (one of the best rooms in New Zealand), concert chamber, banquet hall, restaurant and meeting rooms — in a Modernist palette of concrete, timber and plate glass, with brass fittings, a copper roof and Carrara marble, sparingly used. Warren's design skills were complemented by Maurice Mahoney's talent for detailing and documentation, builder Chas Luney's experience of construction in Christchurch, and Harold Marshall's mastery of acoustics. The project was the making of Marshall (b.1931), whose international career as a concert hall acoustician culminated in his work on the Paris Philharmonie (Jean Nouvel, 2015). The Town Hall was severely damaged in the 2010–2011 earthquakes but, thanks to a victory of local democracy, was restored by Warren and Mahoney Architects instead of being replaced, as Earthquake Recovery Minister Gerry Brownlee preferred. The building now sits on an 850-millimetre concrete raft slab, which is itself supported by more than a thousand concrete piles injected or 'jet grouted' 8 metres into the ground.

Christchurch Town Hall, Kilmore Street.

St Mary's Convent (Rose) Chapel

866 Colombo Street

S & A Luttrell, 1911
Historic Place Category 2

St Mary's Convent Chapel is the surviving building of a Catholic enclave established in Anglican Christchurch in the late nineteenth century. The chapel, now deconsecrated and operated as a venue for hire, was testament to the drive and determination of Irish nun Margaret Boland — Mother Mary Mechtilde (or Mechtildes), to use her Sisters of Mercy religious name — who bought land on Colombo Street in the 1890s and built a convent and school. When the sisters had saved enough to add a chapel, Mother Mary Mechtilde knew what she wanted: something like the chapel at her order's convent in Birmingham, designed by the Gothic Revival architect Augustus Pugin (1812–1852), and featuring windows made by one of Pugin's favourite craftmakers, the Hardman & Co stained glass works.

The chapel was designed by the practice of Australian-born brothers Sidney and Alfred Luttrell, which became a preferred supplier to the Christchurch Catholic Diocese and, quite compatibly, the horse-racing industry. (Sidney Luttrell was part-owner of the horse that won the 1916 Melbourne Cup). The Luttrells had their own construction business and for a while owned a cement company. The architects specified Ōamaru stone and Hoon Hay basalt, and Hardman stained glass windows. The chapel took 12 months to build, and when it opened it was hailed by *The Press* as 'a beautifully finished edifice'. The Catholic bishop congratulated the sisters, in the condescending episcopal tone nuns have long endured: 'with the limited means at their disposal they have devotedly carried out their object'. The chapel narrowly escaped demolition after the Sisters of Mercy quit the site in 1993, and was badly damaged in the 2011 earthquake. Dave Pearson Architects put the building back together again, sensitively restoring its elements, including the rose window from which the chapel takes its current name.

St Mary's Apartments

868 Colombo Street

Peter Beaven, 1997

Memorable architectural encounters do not have to involve buildings. For years, one of the best experiences in New Zealand architecture was a conversation with Peter Beaven (1925–2012). Beaven was eloquent and opinionated but sufficiently reasonable — when not on a public stage — to inoculate his pronouncements with a nuanced subtext. He didn't like Modernism, but distinguished between doctrinaire Le Corbusier and humanist Alvar Aalto; he often opposed schemes championed by his Christchurch contemporary Miles Warren, but always acknowledged Warren's design talent; he disdained privilege, but recognised its advantages — his time at Christ's College taught him, he said, that 'you could do what you liked as long as you did it with panache'.

What Beaven really liked, and advocated for, was the architectural tradition of Christchurch, and in particular the work of Benjamin Mountfort. 'Without him I wouldn't live in Christchurch,' he said, and he meant it. Beaven's office was in Mountfort's Provincial Government Buildings (see pages 98–99); after the building collapsed in the 2011 earthquake (with him in it), Beaven left the city. Thankfully, his St Mary's Apartments, named for the convent that formerly occupied the site, survived the quake. In its design, the 72-unit complex alludes to the quadrangles and steep roofs of Canterbury College (the Arts Centre) and Christ's College; in its structure, it refers to the concrete blockwork popularised in Warren's early architecture; in its layout, it demonstrates Beaven's command of multi-unit planning. And in its effect, it captures the spirit of the 'townscape' principles of one of Beaven's heroes, the English architect and urban designer Gordon Cullen (1914–1994). Where Corbusier, a European Cartesian, thought places should be shaped by rational planning, Cullen believed they should be enjoyed as a sequence of different experiences. At St Mary's Apartments, that's what Beaven aimed for — intrigue, around every corner.

Knox Church

Corner Bealey Avenue and Victoria Street

Robert William England, 1902;
Wilkie + Bruce Architects, 2014
Historic Place Category 2

Following the earthquakes of 2010 and 2011, hundreds of damaged historic buildings in Christchurch were demolished with an alacrity that heritage advocates condemned as opportunism. However, not all owners of distressed old buildings reached for the wrecker's ball; many committed to salvage solutions that ranged from partial restoration to total reconstruction. Knox Church as it now exists is near the latter end of this conservation spectrum.

The Presbyterian church, which opened in 1902, was a brick and stone building designed in the Gothic Revival style by Robert William England, a talented architectural all-rounder who designed commercial buildings, Protestant churches and significant private houses. Around the time of the design of Knox Church, or shortly after, England was joined in his firm by his younger brother Edward Herbert, who continued the practice after Robert's death in 1908. (See the A. J. White's building, pages 118–19.)

The exterior of Knox Church was badly damaged in the 2011 earthquake and subsequently deconstructed. With its outside gone, the building's surviving interior woodwork — dark and rich — was revealed for all to see, and for several years the rimu roof trusses, beams and columns supporting the church's many gables made for a spectacular revelation of Gothicness. In this condition, the building made an evocative ruin, but of course the Presbyterians wanted to return their flagship church to its function. Wilkie + Bruce Architects (design architect Alun Wilkie, 1949–2017) retained the wonderful interior, wrapping it in a pointy-gabled copper and glass shell, supported by concrete buttresses and topped with a corrugated steel roof.

Dorset Street Flats

2–16 Dorset Street

Miles Warren, 1957
Historic Place Category 1

In 1957 the Dorset Street Flats, whose reputation is inversely proportional to its scale, announced the architectural arrival of Miles Warren and declared his design intentions. When he designed the flats, Warren was in his mid-twenties, and not long returned from a couple of years abroad, during which he worked in the Le Corbusier-influenced housing section of London County Council's architecture department. He also visited Modernist pilgrimage sites such as Gunnar Asplund and Sigurd Lewerentz's Woodland Cemetery (1940) in Stockholm, and Corb's Unité d'Habitation (1952) in Marseilles, the apartment building whose rough-cast concrete, or 'béton brut', structure spawned the ultimately unfortunate term 'Brutalism'. Warren was primed for a breakout project; with the Dorset Street Flats, he was to write, 'I was able to put my theories into practice and stuff the design full of everything I knew.'

The building could be called a pioneering work of bachelor Modernism. Warren developed the flats with three male friends, all at the time single, on a rectangular site with a 35-metre street frontage, a two-storey building with two offset groups of four single-level flats. There was a flat for each of the project partners and four for letting; upper-level flats got a balcony and ground-floor units a garden. The essence of the building, Warren wrote, was the use of solid masonry walls, made of load-bearing concrete blocks, soon to be a Warren and Christchurch design trope, instead of the timber framing typical of New Zealand's domestic architecture. The flats were basically 45-square-metre boxes; in their well-detailed interiors, the concrete of blocks and beams was left exposed in an expression of Modernist material honesty. To Warren's delight, the Dorset Street Flats, their roofs low-pitched and eave-less, were sufficiently transgressive to be locally notorious. Now celebrated, they were restored by Young Architects in 2021.

Victoria Clock Tower

Victoria Street and Montreal Street

Benjamin Mountfort, 1860
(addition of base 1897; relocated 1930)
Historic Place Category 1

In the late 1850s, Christchurch's great Gothic Revival architect Benjamin Mountfort designed a clock tower to sit on top of the first section of his Canterbury Provincial Government Buildings (see pages 98–99) on Durham Street. The problem was that the tower was made of iron and the building was made of wood. When the clock tower, packed into 147 boxes, arrived in New Zealand in 1860 from the Coventry foundry of Francis Skidmore (1817–1896) — an accomplished Gothic Revival metalworker — it was obviously too heavy to take its appointed place. The tower, without its clock, subsequently spent decades in a council storage yard until the city's leaders, in a typical colonial marriage of patriotism and pragmatism, re-purposed it as a monument marking the 1897 Diamond Jubilee of Queen Victoria.

Local architecture practice Strouts and Ballantyne designed a stone base for the tower which, finally reunited with its clock, was erected on the corner of Manchester, High and Lichfield streets. On this site the tower later became a traffic hazard, and in 1930, after rejecting an offer from Hamilton City Council to buy it, Christchurch City Council moved it to its present location, where it was restored after the 2011 earthquake. (The earthquake had stopped the time on the clock's face at 12.51.) Restoration work included the diversion of the artesian well discovered under the tower. Unfortunately, at some time in its history the tower lost the gold leaf that originally covered its wrought iron railings.

Peterborough
(Former Teachers' Training College)

Corner Peterborough Street and Montreal Street

George Penlington, 1930
Historic Place Category 2

Architecture can defy geology — the Colosseum was built on a
marsh, with a foundation of Roman concrete (*opus caementicium*),
and has survived for nearly 2000 years — but in doing so can also
tempt fate. As demonstrated in Christchurch's 2010 and 2011
earthquakes, solidity does not necessarily equate with strength;
the impressive mass of the city's neo-Gothic landmarks belied the
instability of the ground beneath them. The building at the corner
of Peterborough and Montreal streets sits heavily on its site — too
heavily, right from the start. A year after its completion in 1930, it
had slumped and cracked, a foreshadowing of more serious failure
80 years later. On reflection, it has done well to last so long.

The building was designed by George Penlington (1865–1932),
chief architect of the Canterbury Education Board, as a training
college for primary school teachers, a role it performed until 1978.
A Gothic Revival building designed in the late 1920s is clearly a case
of design atavism, an untethering of form from meaning as obvious
as the degeneration, 40 years later, of Modernism from movement
to style. Penlington followed the design precedent of nearby Gothic
Revival educational buildings such as the Normal School (now
demolished) and Christ's College: the wings of the Training College,
clad in grey Halswell and cream Ōamaru stone, form a U-shape
around a courtyard, meeting at the building's angled corner entrance
in a medievalist concoction of octagonal battlemented towers
and an oriel and rose window, centred on a 4-metre-high wooden
door seemingly intended to resist battering rams. In the 1980s and
1990s the building was a cultural centre before being converted into
apartments by Fulton Ross Team Architects. (A subterranean carpark
was wrested from the 'wet porridge' of the swampy ground.) The
quake-damaged building has stood empty since 2012, but may be
restored by its developer owner.

Cathedral Grammar Junior School

2 Chester Street West

Andrew Barrie Lab and Tezuka Architects, 2016

Andrew Barrie is that rare figure in New Zealand architecture: a full-time academic who also practises (see also pages 158–59). Barrie teaches at the University of Auckland School of Architecture and Planning, where he is a professor, and carries out his design work under the auspices of his studio, Andrew Barrie Lab. He is, as well, a prolific architectural writer, and his curatorial work includes exhibitions at the Venice Architecture Biennale. After completing his doctoral studies in Tokyo, Barrie worked in the office of the eminent Japanese architect Toyo Ito. He has maintained his Japanese connections and teamed up with Takaharu and Yui Tezuka of Tezuka Architects to design the junior school (years 1–3) for the Cathedral Grammar School, a Church of England school founded in 1881.

Tezuka Architects received international acclaim — and the attention of the Cathedral Grammar School board — for their Fuji Kindergarten (Tokyo, 2007), which features a large oval roof deck on which children can play and run. A roof deck is also incorporated into Cathedral Grammar Junior School, which was conceived as a 'garden school' with an internal layout allowing for both discrete and open-plan teaching spaces. The building's structural design draws on Barrie's research into innovative timber construction materials and technologies. Laminated veneer lumber (LVL) posts and beams slot precisely together after being cut with computer numerical control (CNC) machines to a tolerance of half a millimetre over 12 metres.

ROUTE 6: ILAM CAMPUS

The main campus of the University of Canterbury is a bit out of the way — although just 15 minutes from the city centre by bus — but is worth a visit for its collection of extant Modernist buildings. The university decamped from the city to green fields on the then urban edge 60 years ago. It was a time when Modernist planning and Brutalist architecture promised to be the means to realise a brave new world. Miles Warren's College House is a masterpiece of New Zealand Modernism, and Ilam campus also features strong work by other mid-century Christchurch architects and the concrete-mad Ministry of Works. Several buildings demonstrate the very different current approaches to university architecture.

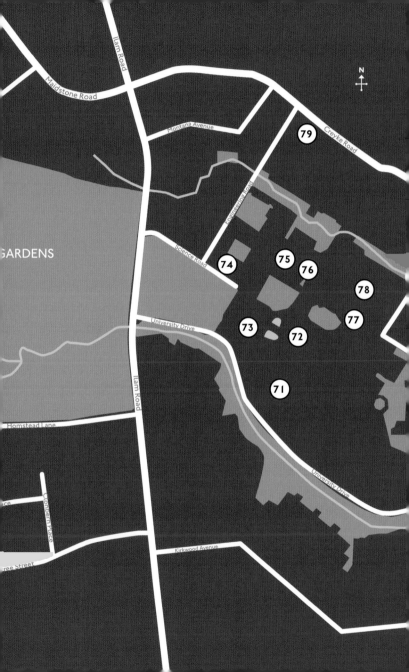

Ilam Campus, University of Canterbury

The Ilam campus of the University of Canterbury represents one of the most pronounced shifts in New Zealand architectural history: a pivot from Mountfortian Gothic Revivalism to Corbusian Modernism. In 1949, after several years of rapid roll growth, Canterbury College, as the public university was then known, decided to move from the inner city to the western fringe of suburbia. Since the late nineteenth century, the College had been housed in the cluster of Gothic Revival buildings that now constitute the Christchurch Arts Centre (see pages 16–35). The new location was a 76-hectare site 5 kilometres away. Architectural responsibility for the redevelopment was assigned to the office of the Government Architect, which for most of the 1950s was led by Gordon Wilson (1900–1959), a key figure in New Zealand Modernist architecture. After Wilson's death, much of the design responsibility for the Ilam campus was assumed by Assistant Government Architect, and later Government Architect, John Blake-Kelly (1913–1988).

The migration to Ilam was from an Oxbridge collegiate arrangement of buildings, more a matter of sympathetic accretion than master-planning zeal (although Samuel Hurst Seager imposed some clarity on the composition, see pages 96–97), to a campus layout guided by Modernist zoning principles that grouped buildings by function: teaching, dwelling, social life. The result, from the early 1960s to the mid-1970s, under Blake-Kelly's leadership, was a flourishing of concrete Brutalism on the flat, green fields of Canterbury, very similar to the development model pursued by the new provincial universities of post-war Britain. Brutalism is history now, but Ilam's Modernist buildings still make strong statements and a challenge for contemporary architects in how to respond to them.

College House

Warren and Mahoney, 1965–1970
Historic Place Category I

In 1964 Miles Warren received a brief for a new project: 'a college for 120 men'. It wasn't a lot to go on, but from it came one of the outstanding works in New Zealand architecture. As Warren later wrote, the key word in the economical instruction was 'college'. The Anglican student hall of residence was not to be a mere dormitory, but rather a complete community, with bedrooms, common rooms and dining hall, and later a chapel and library. So, no march of rooms along either side of a corridor, with toilets at the end. Instead: eight three-storey 'sets' with five bedrooms on each floor, all grouped around a staircase. These sets flank two sides — five on one side, three on the other — of an Oxbridge-style quadrangle closed at opposite ends by the dining hall and library; the chapel pushes into the quad on its three-set side.

College House is a product of what Warren called modern architecture's 'constructivist' phase, a term that evokes the spectre of Bolshevik machine-age art and architecture. This was perhaps not quite what Christ's College old boy Warren had in mind, but you can see what he was getting at. With its programmatic clarity and disciplined and frugal deployment of straightforward materials and fittings — load-bearing concrete blocks, fair-face concrete, timber beams, plywood, Rietveld-like furniture — College House combines the key Modernist precept, form follows function, with Warren's particular brand of explicatory Brutalism. Constructionalism, you could call it, with a side-order of homage in the Gothic allusion of the pointy M-shaped copper roofs of the chapel and library, and the references in the trusses and beams of the chapel to Cecil Wood's Memorial Dining Room at Christ's College (see pages 58–59).

College House, University of Canterbury, Ilam campus.

The dining hall at College House.

Angus Tait Building

Hall and Mackenzie, 1966

The Computer Centre, now re-named for electronics pioneer Angus Tait (1919–2017), was designed to house a telephone exchange and a computer (just the one, big and slow, as computers were, nearly 60 years ago). In comparison with its Brutalist campus siblings it is a modest and graceful building — you could even say it was better than it needed to be (a sure test for good architecture). The building is real Modernists' Modernism: propped up on piers, with a cantilever, a butterfly roof and sun-shading concrete fins on the long elevations. On its greenfield site, the Computer Centre looked fresh and very contemporary when completed, and it retains much of its distinction in what has become a more crowded context.

The building was designed by the practice of Humphrey Hall (1912–1988) and Keith Hamilton Mackenzie (1920–1987). The prominence of Warren and Mahoney has overshadowed other Christchurch Modern-era practices; the firm of Hall and Mackenzie doesn't deserve obscurity. Unlike Christchurch architects of an earlier generation, and some of their peers, who were stylistically heterodox, Hall and Mackenzie seem to have spent their careers as faithful Modernists. Hall designed for himself, when still in his twenties, and after some time spent working in London, one of the first truly Modernist houses in New Zealand, the Corbusian Humphrey Hall House (1938) in Tīmaru. After the war, several years of which Lieutenant Hall spent in prisoner-of-war camps in Italy and Germany, he was in practice for a decade with Paul Pascoe, and then with Keith Mackenzie, who had spent his early twenties commanding a naval patrol boat in the Pacific theatre of war.

Puaka–James Hight Building

Government Architect's Office, MoW, 1974

The 11-storey Brutalist behemoth that is the Puaka–James Hight Building is, at 53 metres high, the tallest building on the Ilam campus, and one of the heftiest extant examples of the mid-century concrete Modernism of the Ministry of Works (MoW). It was designed as the University of Canterbury's main library and it continues to serve that function, although it has always housed other university departments and services as well. The building, initially named for humanities professor and university administrator James Hight (1870–1958) and latterly given the Māori name for Rigel, the brightest star in the Orion constellation, was commissioned from the MoW in 1963. Typically, construction was delayed as the government reshuffled its spending priorities. Local builder Charles Luney (1905–2006) — Modernism's maker in Christchurch — got started in 1969, and the building finally opened in 1974. John Blake-Kelly had overall responsibility in the Government Architect's Office for Ilam campus through the 1960s, but Roger Warr (1931–2011) seems to have led the James Hight project.

Like any sizeable Brutalist building, Puaka–James Hight is confronting, and there have been attempts to use planting to soften its appearance. In the 1980s, ivy was grown on Ilam's Brutalist façades, against the inclinations of the grounds superintendent who noted that the whole point of Brutalism was to see the concrete. At Puaka–James Hight, the cover-up was discontinued when ivy grew into the heating ducts. The post-earthquake rehabilitation of the Puaka–James Hight Building included an extensive re-working of the undercroft by Warren and Mahoney Architects (2013).

Matariki (Registry)

Hall and Mackenzie, 1974

Aside from College House, the Registry building — now called
Matariki, the Māori name for the Pleiades star cluster and also
for the New Year in the Māori lunar calendar — might be the
outstanding work of Modernist architecture on the Ilam campus.
The west face of the building is especially compelling. Thin pillars
of concrete, more fins than columns, exaggerate the height of the
building beyond its six storeys, and are complemented by tall trees
rising from the lawn. The composition shows how good Brutalist
buildings can look in a park setting. Sections of the top floor, which
houses the offices of university administrators, project from the
building like bartizan turrets on medieval castles.

These features, and the general staunchness of the Registry
building, have encouraged conjecture that the building was
designed as a fortress to repel student invaders. This seems
improbable — the University of Canterbury campus in the early
1970s was hardly the Sorbonne in May 1968 — although students
have staged the occasional occupation over the years.

The Registry demonstrates Hall and Mackenzie's mastery
of concrete design, the signature characteristic of the so-called
Christchurch School over the two decades from the late 1950s.
Like other Brutalist work on the Ilam campus, the building
could be viewed as an in-your-face proclamation of local
architectural ability on the campus of a university that never
established a School of Architecture. The Registry was badly
damaged in the 2011 earthquake; structural remediation and
internal 'modernisation' was supervised by Warren and Mahoney
Architects (2014).

Jack Erskine Building

Architectus, with Cook Sargisson Hitchcock and Royal Associates, 1998

When it opened in 1998, the Mathematics, Statistics and Computer Sciences Building, now named for scientist and engineer Jack Erskine (1872–1960), was the best work of architecture at Ilam since College House. It probably still is. In its materials and their monumental deployment, it relates to the Modernist buildings constructed in the first 20 years of the campus's development, but if architecture is a dialogue, you could say the Maths, Stats and Computer Sciences Building significantly advanced the conversation.

The building was designed by a team led by Architectus, a practice established in Auckland in the late 1980s by Patrick Clifford, Malcolm Bowes and Michael Thomson (see also pages 104–05, 108–09, 134–35 and 142–49). It is tempting to see in the building a fusion of two architectural traditions: the post-war, temperate-climate architecture of Auckland, thinner skinned and more open to the natural environment; and the heavier architecture of Christchurch, thick-walled and more protected against a less amenable climate.

In its legible distinction between three north-facing, seven-storey towers housing staff offices, a four-storey teaching wing to the south, and the circulation areas connecting them, the building is a model of clarity; its refinement stands out against its Brutalist forebears like a pin-striped suit among rugby-jersey hoops. Architectural spectators of the building will appreciate a separation of 'served' and 'servant' spaces typical of the work of the great American architect Louis Kahn (1901–1974), an acknowledged influence on the work of Architectus. For their part, inhabitants of the building have had reason to be grateful for its efficient environmental performance.

Ernest Rutherford Building

Jasmax, 2018

What do buildings say about the practices that design them? Over the past 20 years, Jasmax and Warren and Mahoney Architects have emerged as New Zealand's two largest architectural firms, with offices in several cities around the country and also in Australia. Jasmax originated and is still concentrated in Auckland; Warren and Mahoney expanded from its Christchurch base.

Without engaging in geographical determinism, it is possible to discern in the practices' architecture traits associated with their places of origin. While Jasmax is increasingly corporate, the firm's architecture traditionally has been more relaxed than that of Warren and Mahoney, which is given to producing assertive and even dominating buildings. Jasmax hasn't had a house style, but in the four decades following its foundation in 1963 its work was characterised by a kind of humanism that has softened the hard edges of modern architecture. Conveniently, the firms' cultural differences are illustrated by adjacent terminals at Christchurch Airport: one hard and bright, by Warren and Mahoney (with Australian firm Hassell); the other more layered and subdued, by Jasmax (with Australian firm BVN).

Jasmax's approach suits the recent vogue for flexible commercial and education spaces — the two genres are now almost interchangeable — and is represented on the Ilam campus by the sciences building named for Canterbury University's most famous alumnus, nuclear physicist Ernest Rutherford (1871–1937). The key to the building's planning is the grand atrium, which is all about ascent, literally and metaphorically — the design is intended to evoke the journey of the mythical figure Tāwhaki, who climbed into the heavens in search of celestial knowledge.

Beatrice Tinsley Building

**Jasmax, DJRD Architects
and Royal Associates Architects, 2019**

After the Christchurch earthquakes, it seemed popular sentiment
for change would find profound structural expression, both at the
scale of individual buildings and of the city. It hasn't really worked
out that way. New buildings are far more resilient than their pre-
quake predecessors, and there has been little appetite for high-
rise habitation in what was anyway a comparatively low-rise city.
But while many new buildings in Christchurch look different from
their pre-quake antecedents, they don't look much different
from new buildings in other places, or from each other, and the
procrustean planning regime — Modernism redux, with zones recast
as 'precincts' — imposed by the recovery authority foreclosed the
possibilities of new paradigms of urban development.

The story of post-quake, non-residential timber construction
in Christchurch shows how hard it can be to give architectural
realisation to ideas whose time would seem to have come. You
would think timber might indeed be the natural choice for the
rebuilding of a New Zealand city: intuitively, it seems 'safe'; it is a
plentiful and sustainable material; and builders in Aotearoa New
Zealand have worked with it for centuries. Also, in Christchurch,
the University of Canterbury carries out world-leading research in
timber engineering.

But the gap between technological understanding, on the
one hand, and manufacturing and building capability and political
commitment, on the other, means large-scale timber structures
are rather like demonstration models. One such exemplar is the
Ilam building named for acclaimed astronomer and cosmologist
Beatrice Tinsley (1941–1981). The four-storey building uses
laminated veneer lumber (LVL) beams, 'moment-framed' and
cross-braced, to provide flexible resistance to severe seismic
movement. The re-use of the existing foundations and basement
level enhances the building's sustainable credentials.

Jane Soons Building

Government Architect's Office, MoW, c1975–1976

It's strange that a building so solidly present on the ground is so sketchily present in the records. The building now named for Jane Soons (1931–2020), an eminent geomorphologist who, when appointed to a chair in geography in 1971 became the University of Canterbury's first female professor, was constructed a decade and a half into the university's progressive occupation of the Ilam campus. With its Jenga-like protruding beams and appended external staircase, the five-storey concrete building — a penthouse level was a later addition — is so reductionist an expression of the Brutalist architecture of the Ministry of Works in its 1970s heyday as to be almost a caricature. The geography department's building was one arm of a tripartite arrangement of connected structures, in the shape of half a swastika, that also housed the sociology and psychology departments in the arts or humanities precinct of the campus.

Considering the scope of the Ilam project and their own scale, the arts buildings received surprisingly little critical contemporary attention. Admittedly, there were very few New Zealand publications interested in architecture, but perhaps there was also a sense that Ilam had become a rote roll-out of a design style that had become mundane and certainly not crowd-pleasing. Anyone in search of architectural excitement in the mid-1970s looked to Wellington, and the playful and surprising buildings of Ian Athfield and Roger Walker. Government Architect John Blake-Kelly (1913–1988) was defensive in the face of such intimations of post-Modernism, telling an architects' conference in 1973 that he had 'no time for an architecture that spews its building services entrails seeking some gimmick popularity'. Blake-Kelly was clear that the Ministry of Works' buildings 'are for client departments . . . not for us'. His silence about the buildings' actual inhabitants reveals the tragedy of Modernism: architects designing for the people had become bureaucrats designing for other bureaucrats.

Rehua

Athfield Architects, 2019

The 150-year evolution of the University of Canterbury is clearly expressed in three main waves of construction. The first realised the foundational Gothic Revival buildings on the city site of what was then Canterbury College, and the second brought mid-twentieth-century Brutalism to the new greenfield campus in suburban Ilam. Styles had changed, although building functionality was not so different. University education in the 1960s and 1970s was still a matter of remote figures descending from their offices to appear at lecterns in front of serried ranks of more or less attentive students; university buildings were organised to facilitate this hierarchical form of knowledge dissemination. (Brutalism proclaimed institutional authority as loudly as Gothic Revivalism, but without the charm.) In the contemporary academy, this approach is passé; a devolution in learning responsibility has prioritised peer collaboration, and the provision of spaces that encourage active engagement. The latest generation of Ilam buildings promote movement and informal encounters; this is an architecture of atriums and mezzanines, hubs, pods and casual meeting areas.

Rehua, like the Ernest Rutherford and Beatrice Tinsley Buildings (see pages 198–99 and 200–01), epitomises the new orthodoxy. The building, which bears the Māori name for Antares, the brightest star in the constellation of Scorpius, is a comprehensive reconstruction of the earthquake-damaged Commerce Building (1996). Athfield Architects designed the original seven-storey concrete slab building at the height of their expressive phase, which notably yielded Wellington Central Library (1992), and they returned for the do-over. If any practice is attuned to universities' current spatial preferences, it's Athfield Architects; the atrium in the Commerce Building, for example, prefigured the current vogue for this building feature. Re-clad in terracotta and internally lined with poutama-patterned panels, Rehua is a busy building which retains some formal connection to the peak exuberance of Athfield Architects' post-Modernism.

John Britten Building

69 Creyke Road, Ilam

Warren and Mahoney Architects, 2009

From its inception in the late 1950s, Warren and Mahoney has been an ambitious firm, its competitiveness propelled by the drive of Miles Warren, just as its path to success was smoothed by his charm. After Warren's retirement in 1994, shortly after the departure of fellow practice founder Maurice Mahoney, the firm went through a period of reformation and renewal, emerging in the early 2000s with a sharpened corporate focus. Warren and Mahoney's next-generation confidence was expressed in its architecture. In buildings ranging from houses to offices and schools, Warren and Mahoney's work became characterised by a neo-Modernist rectilinearity, a hard-edged architecture of steel, glass and concrete. (After half a century, Brutalism was still in the blood.) Warren and Mahoney's architecture is not tentative or whimsical; it's tempting to interpret the practice's many cantilevers as assertions of its brand. Very deliberately, the practice configured itself for inter-operability with corporate and institutional clients; it connects to power with the precision of a supply ship docking with a space station.

A few years before the Christchurch earthquakes, Warren and Mahoney designed for the University of Canterbury an engineering research building on the eastern edge of the Ilam campus. The building, now named for Christchurch mechanical engineer and innovative motorcycle designer John Britten (1950–1995), is a two-level container — cantilevered, naturally — of flexible display and work spaces. On its street face, a skin of fritted glass promotes thermal performance and provides aesthetic distinction. The building is the epitome of what architect and writer David Mitchell famously called an 'elegant shed'. (The still-resonant phrase was the title of a 1984 book and television series by Mitchell.) More heroically, critic Andrew Paul Wood likened it to one of the great works of European Modernism, the Bauhaus building at Dessau, designed in the mid-1920s by Walter Gropius (1883–1969).

ARCHITECTURAL STYLES AND INFLUENCES

Alvar Aalto (1898–1976): Influential Finnish architect and designer whose Modernist buildings exhibit humane qualities and were realised as 'total works of art'; that is, he and his first wife, Aino Aalto (1894–1949), would design not only a building but also its fittings and furniture.

Art Deco: Architectural and design style popular in the 1920s and 1930s that took its name from the 1925 Exposition Internationale des Arts Décoratifs et Industriels Modernes in Paris. In architecture, Art Deco was a highly stylised version of Modernism that blended sleek forms, contemporary materials and bold colours to self-consciously glamorous effect.

Arts and Crafts: Design philosophy and practice that emerged in Britain in the mid-nineteenth century and was influential in the decades prior to the First World War. Arts and Crafts architecture evoked the organic nature and functional simplicity of pre-Industrial Age architecture and, as its name suggests, promoted handcrafted construction and the 'honest' use of natural materials.

Augustus Pugin (1812–1852): English architect, designer and critic who was a pioneer of the Gothic Revival. A Catholic convert, he designed many churches, both Anglican and Catholic, as well as the interior of the Palace of Westminster in London.

Beaux-Arts: The rich, Classically-influenced architectural style promulgated by the École des Beaux-Arts in Paris from the mid-nineteenth century through to the first few decades of the twentieth century.

Brutalism: Term coined in Britain in the early 1950s — derived from 'béton brut' (raw concrete) — to characterise the Modernist architecture of Le Corbusier and applied to monolithic poured-concrete buildings with clearly expressed or emphasised structural elements. The style, also known as 'New Brutalism', endured in New Zealand until the end of the 1970s.

Classical architecture or Classicism: The revival of, or reference to, Greek or Roman architecture of classical antiquity. A serious architecture of pedestals, columns and pediments, and comparative decorative restraint.

Collegiate Gothic: Sub-genre of Gothic Revival architecture popular in the late nineteenth and early twentieth centuries on school and university campuses. The historicist style blended Gothic and Tudor elements and often favoured a more horizontal expression of Gothic Revival's vertical or 'pointy' forms.

Edwin Lutyens (1869–1944): Celebrated as the leading English architect of his time. A traditionalist who was adept at adapting to contemporary establishment taste, he won numerous commissions for country houses and war memorials, and played an important part in the design of New Delhi.

Frank Gehry (1929–): Canadian-born American architect who is famous for such virtuoso designs as the Guggenheim Bilbao (1997), Walt Disney Concert Hall (Los Angeles, 2003) and his own post-Modern house in Santa Monica (California, 1978). Now so famous he is a corporate brand.

Frank Lloyd Wright (1867–1959): The greatest American architect, some claim, of all time. In a 70-year career lived in the public gaze, Wright designed hundreds of buildings and championed his 'organic' brand of modern architecture. Fallingwater (Mill Run, Pennsylvania, 1937) is hailed as one of the best-ever works of American architecture; other significant Wright buildings are the Robie Residence (Chicago, Illinois, 1909), Taliesin West (Scottsdale, Arizona, 1937) and the Solomon R. Guggenheim Museum (New York, 1959).

George Gilbert Scott, senior (1811–1878): Prolific English Gothic Revival architect. Churches and cathedrals — including ChristChurch Cathedral in New Zealand — were his specialties, although he also designed workhouses, asylums and such prominent secular structures as the Midland Grand Hotel at St Pancras Station (London, 1873) and the Albert Memorial (London,

1876). His two sons, George Gilbert Scott Jr (1839–1897) and John Oldrid Scott (1841–1913), were also architects, as was, more successfully, his grandson Sir Giles Gilbert Scott (1880–1960).

Gerrit Rietveld (1888–1964): Dutch architect and furniture designer; in both fields he focused on inexpensive production methods, new materials, prefabrication and standardisation, and to this day architects are covetous of his chair designs, especially that icon of Modernist design, the Red and Blue Chair (1917).

Gothic Revival: The nineteenth-century revival, associated in Britain with High Church Anglicanism and Roman Catholicism, of the Gothic architectural style dominant in much of late medieval Europe. The Gothic style was an architecture of pointy bits — spires, flying buttresses, steep gables, rib vaults and lancet windows. Gothic Revivalism came to Christchurch with the Anglican settlers of the Canterbury Association, and held sway for the first 50 years of the city's history.

Italianate, Italian Renaissance, Italian Villa: Synonymous terms for the picturesque adaptation of the Italian Renaissance Villa type popular in nineteenth-century Britain, especially among nouveau riche bourgeois clients; the style spread to the British Empire and North America, where it lingered until the end of the century.

Jacobethan or Jacobethan Revival: Term originated in the 1930s by English poet John Betjeman to describe a nineteenth-century revival style that combined elements of Elizabethan and Jacobean architecture. Features included wide 'Tudor' arches, steep gables, porches, parapets and chimneys, and lighter stone surrounds for doors and windows.

Le Corbusier, born Charles-Édouard Jeanneret (1887–1965): Swiss-born architect, planner and polemicist who was probably the most famous architect of the twentieth century; designer of such canonical Modernist works as the Villa Savoye near Paris, Notre-Dame du Haut chapel at Ronchamps and the city of Chandigarh in northern India.

Louis Kahn (1901–1974): American architect celebrated for designing buildings of monumental presence and authority such as the Salk Institute (La Jolla, California, 1959), National Assembly

Building of Bangladesh (Dhaka, 1962), Phillips Exeter Academy Library (Exeter, New Hampshire, 1965) and Kimbell Art Museum (Fort Worth, Texas, 1966).

Ludwig Mies van der Rohe (1886–1969): One of the outstanding twentieth-century architects. Born in Germany, he designed one of the great early Modernist buildings, the Barcelona Pavilion (1929), and taught at the Bauhaus before moving in the late 1930s to America, where he designed the equally acclaimed Farnsworth House (Plano, Illinois, 1951) and Seagram Building (New York, 1958).

Maya Lin (1959–): American artist and designer who was 21 years old when she won the 1981 competition to design the Vietnam Veterans Memorial in Washington DC, a project that has had a huge influence on memorial design around the world.

Moderne: Also called Streamline Moderne, a toned-down iteration of Art Deco that emerged in the 1930s and was characterised by curved forms and horizontal lines, and often by ship-like styling and nautical elements.

Modernism: The most important architectural style or movement of the twentieth century. Modernism was characterised by a rejection of ornamentation, the belief that a building's form should follow from an analysis of its function, and a commitment to the rational use of contemporary industrial materials and building technologies. In New Zealand, after a slow start, Modernism was the architectural orthodoxy from the Second World War to the end of the 1970s.

Neo-Georgian: Revival in early twentieth-century Britain, and therefore in New Zealand, of the architectural style in vogue under the Hanoverian monarchs, Georges I to IV (spanning 1714–1830). A restrained style, both in its original as well as its revived iterations, characterised by symmetry, balance and proportion. Brick and stone were materials typical of the style.

Palazzo: A style of late nineteenth- and early twentieth-century building based on the town houses (palazzi) of Italian Renaissance patrician families. The building type — solid and symmetrical, and more austere than buildings in 'Italian Villa' mode — was particularly popular with late Victorian London gentlemen's clubs.

Queen Anne Revival: A late nineteenth- and early twentieth-century historicist architectural style that referred very loosely to the English Baroque style popular in the reign of Queen Anne (1702–1714). Features could include gables, turrets and fine brickwork with bands of masonry detailing.

Richard Cromwell Carpenter (1812–1855): English architect who, as a member of the Ecclesiological Society, was closely involved with the Gothic Revival and in particular its application to Anglican church buildings.

Romanesque: Pre-Gothic style of medieval architecture featuring semi-circular arches for windows and doors, vaults to support the roof, and massive piers and walls.

Spanish Mission: An early twentieth-century architectural style derived from late eighteenth- and early nineteenth-century Spanish colonial buildings in California. The style, characterised by stucco walls with a curvilinear gable shape or low parapets at the roof line, enjoyed some popularity in New Zealand in the inter-war period.

Toyo Ito (1941–): Japanese architect celebrated for his innovative designs and conceptual approach to his practice; awarded international architecture's leading personal award, the Pritzker Prize, in 2013.

Tudor Revival: An early twentieth-century revival of the late-Gothic architectural style of Tudor England incorporating towers, mock battlements and crenellations, oriel windows, and low 'Tudor' arches that had some popularity as a New World collegiate architectural style. The style's suburban domestic variant communicated antique rusticity through the use of half-timber work and gabled roofs.

Walter Gropius (1883–1969): German architect who was a founder of the short-lived but hugely influential Bauhaus design school and one of the key figures in the development of Modernist architecture. Practised and taught in the United States after he fled from Nazi Germany in the mid-1930s.

GLOSSARY OF ARCHITECTURAL TERMS

Arcuated: Arched, like a bow.

Bartizan: An overhanging, wall-mounted turret projecting from the walls of medieval and early modern fortifications and used for surveillance and defensive purposes.

Buttress: Masonry mass projecting from or built against a wall to provide support; a flying buttress is an arch or half-arch that extends from the upper part of a wall to a pier, again to counter a building's lateral thrust.

Chancel: The space around the altar at the east end of a church, traditionally reserved for the clergy and choir.

Encaustic (tiles): Ceramic tiles into which colours have been set in a heating process.

Entablature: Upper part of a Classical building, supported by columns, and comprising the architrave (the lintel above the columns), frieze (the decorative band above the architrave), and cornice (the horizontal moulding at the top of a building).

Fascine: Decorative element fashioned to resemble a cylindrical bundle of sticks.

Fenestration: The arrangement of windows in a building.

Festoon: Carved building-façade ornament in the form of a ribboned garland of fruit and flowers.

Finial: An ornament, commonly foliated, on the top of a building.

Fritted glass: Glass printed with a ceramic composite that has been fired into an opaque coating.

Hipped roof: A roof that slopes downwards on all four sides towards a building's walls.

Ionic column: One of the three column styles of Greek Classical architecture, more slender than the Doric and less ornate than the Corinthian column.

Moment framing: Structural technique designed to allow a building to withstand seismic shocks. Rigid framing connections are used to lock together a flexible building frame resistant to lateral and overturning forces.

Mullioned: Windows divided by vertical bars or piers, usually made of stone.

Oriel window: A type of bay window that protrudes from the main wall of a building, usually from an upper floor, and is supported by a corbel (a structural element, usually of stone) or bracket.

Parapet: An extension of a wall along the edge of the roof, originally designed for defensive purposes.

Pediment: Classically derived gable, usually triangular in shape, surmounting the entablature of a building above the main entrance.

Pilaster: A protruding rectangular column or pier.

Pilotis: Columns or pillars that support a building, thereby leaving the ground level completely or partially open.

Portico: Covered building entrance, usually in the form of a roof supported by columns.

Poutama: Stepped weaving pattern ('stairway to heaven') used in Māori tukutuku latticework and mats.

Quoin: A dressed stone at the corner of a building.

String course: A decorative horizontal band, usually of brick or stone, on a building façade.

Tourelle: A type of projecting circular turret, supported by corbels or piers; an element typical of French château architecture, nineteenth-century Scottish 'baronial' buildings, and popular for a while in Britain's dominions.

Transepts: Transverse arms of a cross-shaped church; that is, the two areas that flank, on either side, the nave or main body of the building.

Undercroft: Traditionally, a cellar or storage room, often vaulted; in contemporary usage, a ground- or street-level area, open at the side but covered by the building above.

SOURCES AND FURTHER READING

The website (my.christchurchcitylibraries.com) of Christchurch City Council's Libraries is a good source of information about the city's architecture, especially its significant heritage buildings. Council-published booklets about some of these buildings may be downloaded from the site.

Heritage New Zealand Pouhere Taonga, the government heritage agency, lists designated 'historic places' online, often with extensive descriptive text (heritage.org.nz/the-list). The list is dominated by pre-Second World War buildings, but Modern-era architecture is increasingly represented.

Ngā Tāngata Taumata Rau — The Dictionary of New Zealand Biography, itself a part of *Te Ara — The Encyclopedia of New Zealand* (teara.govt.nz), has short biographies of many of the prominent deceased architects who have practised in Christchurch, as noted in the bibliography.

Papers Past (paperspast.natlib.govt.nz) is the National Library's online archive of New Zealand newspapers, which at present covers the period from 1839 to 1961. Newspapers, especially in the later nineteenth and early twentieth centuries, often published detailed accounts of architectural projects, including reports on opening ceremonies. In researching this book, Christchurch newspapers *The Press*, *The Star* and *The Lyttelton Times* were particularly useful.

Anyone wanting to dig deeper into Christchurch's architectural record might explore the architectural drawing collection held at the University of Canterbury's Macmillan Brown Library. The catalogue can be consulted at kohika.canterbury.ac.nz. The website christhurchmodern.co.nz has an illustrated database of mid-twentieth-century Christchurch Modernist houses. Te Kāhui Whaihanga New Zealand Institute of Architects offers a snapshot of recent Christchurch architecture in the awards section of its website (nzia.co.nz).

For those wanting a more visceral encounter with the city's architecture, the non-profit organisation Te Pūtahi Centre for

Architecture and City Making runs the annual Open Christchurch site visit programme (openchch.nz).

As noted in the introduction, architecture has been a hierarchical and gendered profession in New Zealand, as it has been in most places, and unless practitioners were practice partners — and until recently such leaders were nearly always male — they were not written into the record. Redress is provided in *Making Space: A History of New Zealand Women in Architecture*, edited by Elizabeth Cox (Massey University Press, 2022.)

The following publications were helpful in the writing of this book, and are recommended to anyone in search of further reading about its contents.

Barrie, Andrew. *Shigeru Ban: Cardboard Cathedral*. Auckland: Auckland University Press, 2014.

——'Warren and Mahoney in Christchurch I'. Itinerary No. 15, *Block: The Broadsheet of the Auckland Branch of the New Zealand Institute of Architects*, no. 7, 2008.

——'Peter Beaven 1: The 60s & 70s'. Itinerary No. 24, *Block: The Broadsheet of the Auckland Branch of the New Zealand Institute of Architects*, no. 7, 2009.

Beck, Haig and Jackie Cooper, eds. *Architectus: Between Order and Opportunity*. ORO Editions, 2009.

Beaven, Peter. *Peter Beaven: Architect*. Edited by Ian Lochhead. Peter Beaven Architecture, 2016.

Bennet, Barnaby, James Dann, Emma Johnson and Ryan Reynolds, eds. *Once in a Lifetime: City-building After Disaster in Christchurch*. Freerange Press, 2015.

Blundell, Sally. *Ravenscar House: A Biography*. Christchurch: Canterbury University Press, 2022.

Ciaran, Fiona. 'Stained Glass in Canterbury, New Zealand, 1860 to 1988'. PhD thesis, University of Canterbury, 1992.

Cox, Elizabeth, ed. *Making Space: A History of New Zealand Women in Architecture*. Auckland: Massey University Press, 2022.

Gatley, Julia. *Athfield Architects*. Auckland: Auckland University Press, 2012.

——, ed. *Long Live the Modern: New Zealand's New Architecture 1904 –1984*. Auckland: Auckland University Press, 2008.

Helms, Ruth M. 'The Architecture of Cecil Wood'. PhD thesis, University of Canterbury, 1996.

Joiner, Duncan. 'The Government Architect's Office, 1940–1992'. *Tāpoto–The Brief* (New Zealand Institute of Architects) 2, 2019.

Lochhead, Ian. *A Dream of Spires: Benjamin Mountfort and the Gothic Revival*. Christchurch: Canterbury University Press, 1999.

——, ed. *The Christchurch Town Hall 1965–2019*. Christchurch: Canterbury University Press, 2019.

Richardson, Peter. 'Building the Dominion: Government Architecture in New Zealand, 1840–1922'. PhD thesis, University of Canterbury, 1997.

——'The Government Architect's Office, 1869–1940'. *Tāpoto–The Brief* (New Zealand Institute of Architects) 2, 2019.

Shaw, Peter. *A History of New Zealand Architecture*. 3rd ed. Auckland: Hodder Becket Moa Becket Publishers, 2003.

Te Ara —The Encyclopedia of New Zealand. Biographies of: William Barnett Armson (written by Jonathan Mane-Wheoki); Peter Beaven (Ian Lochhead); Maxwell Bury (Anne Marchant); Joseph Clarkson Maddison (John Wilson); James Edward Fitzgerald (W. David McIntyre); William Henry Gummer (Ian Lochhead); Alfred and Sidney Luttrell (Ann McEwan); J. T. Mair (Peter Shaw); Benjamin Mountfort (Ian Lochhead); Paul Pascoe (Ana Robertson); Francis William Petre (Ian Lochhead); Frederick Strouts (Jonathan Mane-Wheoki); Gordon Wilson (Julia Gatley); Cecil Walter Wood (Ruth M. Helms).

Walker, Charles, ed. *Exquisite Apart: 100 Years of Architecture in New Zealand*. Auckland: Balasoglou Books / New Zealand Institute of Architects, 2005.

Walsh, John. 'Canterbury Pilgrim [Peter Beaven]'. *Houses New Zealand* 11, spring 2009: 75–99.

——*Patrick Clifford: New Zealand Institute of Architects Gold Medal 2014*. Auckland: New Zealand Institute of Architects, 2014.

Warren, Miles. *Miles Warren: An Autobiography*. Christchurch: Canterbury University Press, 2008.

Warren and Mahoney. *Warren and Mahoney Architects: 1958–1989*. Warren and Mahoney, 1989.

——*New Territory. Warren and Mahoney: 50 years of New Zealand Architecture*. Balasoglou Books, 2005.

Willis, Gavin, ed. *Selected Architecture Christchurch: A Guide*. Christchurch: The Caxton Press, 2005.

ACKNOWLEDGEMENTS

It has been a pleasure to return to Christchurch two years after the publication of the initial walking guide to the city's architecture and to once more work with Patrick Reynolds on this extensively revised edition of the guide.

We both thank Nicola Legat, publisher at Massey University Press, for her ongoing commitment to publishing New Zealand architecture, and acknowledge the contribution of her colleagues Anna Bowbyes, Anna Jackson-Scott and Emily Goldthorpe. Thanks also to Sjoerd Langeveld for his expert photo finishing, and to designer Imogen Greenfield for her sympathetic layout, attention to detail and map-making skill.

Most of the buildings in this guide were photographed from the street (which is how they will be viewed by the guide's users), but some were captured closer up. For access to grounds and buildings the author and photographer thank the Arts Centre Te Matatiki Toi Ora; Cathedral Grammar Junior School; Christ's College; Christchurch Botanic Gardens Visitor Centre; Christchurch City Libraries; Oxford Terrace Baptist Church; the University of Canterbury; and Vbase (operator of Christchurch Town Hall).

The publication of this guide has been supported by the Warren Trust, which does so much to promote architectural education in Aotearoa New Zealand. The trust's founder, Sir Miles Warren, passed away as this book was being completed; his loss to architecture and his city is as large as the contribution he made during his extraordinary career.

Special thanks to Catherine Hammond, for her encouragement and invaluable research assistance, advice and tolerance, and to Xavier Walsh, for his inspirational insouciance.

INDEX

Architects

Architecture & design practices

First published in 2020 by Massey University Press
This revised edition published 2023
Massey University Press
Private Bag 102904, North Shore Mail Centre
Auckland 0745, New Zealand
www.masseypress.ac.nz

A catalogue record for this book is available from the
National Library of New Zealand

Printed and bound in China by 1010 Printing Asia Ltd

ISBN: 978-1-99-101638-6

The publisher is grateful for the support of
The Warren Trust and Resene

THE WARREN TRUST

the paint the professionals use